SECRETS OF THE RUSSIAN CHESS MASTERS: BOOK 1

Fundamentals of the Game

ALSO BY LEV ALBURT

Comprehensive Chess Course: Volume I
(with Roman Pelts)

Comprehensive Chess Course: Volume II
(with Roman Pelts)

Chess Tactics for the Tournament Player
(Comprehensive Chess Course Series)
(with Sam Palatnik)

The King in Jeopardy
(Comprehensive Chess Course Series)
(with Sam Palatnik)

THE FOUR TITLES ABOVE ARE AVAILABLE FROM W. W. NORTON

Test and Improve Your Chess

ALSO BY LARRY PARR

Viktors Pupols: American Master

The Bobby Fischer I Knew and Other Stories
(with Arnold Denker)

SECRETS OF THE RUSSIAN CHESS MASTERS: BOOK 1

Fundamentals of the Game

Grandmaster Lev Alburt

Larry Parr

W. W. Norton & Company
New York   London

For information about permission to reproduce selections from this book, write to Permissions, W. W. Norton & Company, Inc., 500 Fifth Avenue, New York, NY 10110-0017.

The text of this book is composed in 10/13 Minion. Diagrams are set in Chess Draughts, Linotype Game Pi. The display is set in Helvetica Neue.
Composition and book design by Frank Elley
Manufacturing by The Courier Companies, Inc.

Library of Congress Cataloging-in-Publication Data
Alburt, Lev.
    Secrets of the Russian chess masters / Lev Alburt, Larry Parr.
        p.   cm.
    Includes indexes.
    ISBN 0-393-04115-8 (v. 1). — ISBN 0-393-04116-6 (v. 2)
    1. Chess. 2. Chess players—Russia (Federation) I. Parr, Larry.
II. Title.
GV1449.5.A43 1997
794.1´2—dc21   96–50896
                                                                 CIP

W. W. Norton & Company, Inc., 500 Fifth Avenue, New York, NY 10110-0017
http://www.wwnorton.com
W. W. Norton & Company Ltd., 10 Coptic Street, London WC1A 1PU

1 2 3 4 5 6 7 8 9 0

To my students, who inspired me to write this book
— Lev Alburt

To Lawrence and the late Irene Parr
— Larry Parr

Contents

SECRETS OF THE RUSSIAN CHESS MASTERS: BOOK 1

Fundamentals of the Game

1 *Play Chess in One Hour*

HERE'S THE GOOD NEWS: Chess has fewer rules, which are more easily learned, than many children's board games. By the time you finish this chapter, you will be able to play a game of chess as well or better than many of the 25 million to 30 million Americans who, according to polls, know how to play a game that is also renowned as an art and a sporting competition.

Chess—the royal game and the passion of such geniuses as America's Robert Fischer and Russia's Garry Kasparov—has been called the gymnasium of the mind and, in Goethe's phrase, "the touchstone of the intellect." Youngsters learn logic and discipline when unraveling its intricacies, lengthening their attention spans in the process. The "Chess Makes You Smart" pin can be seen on the T-shirts of thousands of school children at the large scholastic chess competitions held annually throughout the United States. Education researchers confirm what many parents observe: Their kids really do become more focused and curious after learning chess. Grades go up.

Another favorite phrase among chess people is "Chess Is a Game for Life." And for all people, too. Long considered a male preserve, the chess world now contains women grandmasters, including Hungary's fabulous Polgar sisters—Judit, Zsuzsa and Sofia—who have triumphed in competition against the strongest male grandmasters.

As a pastime that will keep the mind active and fit, chess is unrivalled. People in middle age find chess to be a wonderful outlet for both artistic expression and competitive drive; senior citizens use chess to keep their minds sharp through mental exercise and to meet new friends of all ages.

"Chess, like love, like music," wrote Siegbert Tarrasch, a great German master of the early twentieth century, "has the power to make men happy."

That is why we say, "Welcome to chess!"

THE GOAL OF CHESS

The ultimate aim for both players in a chess game is to threaten the inevitable capture of the opponent's King, and the first player to establish such a threat is the winner. If neither player can achieve this goal, the game ends in a draw.

Threatening the inevitable capture of the King is called *checkmate*. We say "inevitable capture" because the King is never actually captured. Checkmate occurs when the King is directly attacked by an enemy man and it is unable to avoid capture on the very next move. The three conditions for checkmate are:

1. The King has no safe move out of the attack.
2. No other friendly piece can block the attack on the King.
3. The enemy man delivering the attack cannot be captured.

Checkmate ends the game without the attacked King actually being removed from the board. Usually, the losing player tips over the checkmated King in sporting recognition of defeat.

In many of the lesser board games, players mindlessly attempt to capture the opponent's pieces or men, and the side that establishes an advantage in brute force wins the game. While the capture of enemy men is also important in chess, it is completely subordinate to the goal of inflicting a checkmate. Having more men may help to deliver checkmate, but there are literally hundreds of millions of instances in chess where the side with more men loses because the "weaker" side delivers mate.

More later about checkmate.

STARTING POSITIONS OF THE PIECES

Diagram 1 shows the starting position for both White and Black. In all chess diagrams, the White side is shown moving up the board and the Black side down the board.

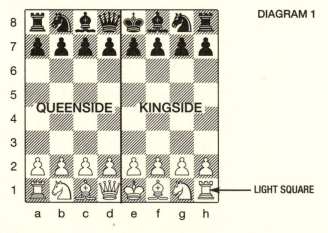

DIAGRAM 1

LIGHT SQUARE

Both sides begin with completely equal forces of 16 men each:

♟ 8   pawns (placed in front of the pieces on the edge of the board)

♜ 2   Rooks (placed in the corners)

♞ 2   Knights (sometimes called horses, placed next to the Rooks)

♝ 2   Bishops (next to the Knights)

♛ 1   Queen (between the Bishops)

♚ 1   King (also between the Bishops)

In this and most other chess books, the phrase *chess piece* or simply *piece* does not include pawns, which are known by their own name or by common literary terms such as "foot soldiers" and "private soldiers," suggestive of diminutive cosmic status.

"Pieces" include the *minor pieces,* the Bishop and Knight, which are so called because of their relative weakness compared with the *major pieces,* the Queen and Rook. The King is also a "piece"—indeed, *the* piece in the sense that its inevitable capture, or checkmate, is the goal of every chess game.

Note two little tricks in the starting position shown in Diagram 1 on page 12 :

1. Brand into your consciousness right now that the White Queen starts on a light-colored square and the Black Queen on a dark-colored square. Here's a memory aid: "The Queen starts on its own color."

2. Imagine that Diagram 1 is actually a real chess board (and all chess boards—like this diagram—have 64 squares) placed on a table, and you are sitting behind the White pieces and the opponent behind the Black pieces. There is a light-colored square in the right-hand corner of the board as you face it and in the right-hand corner of the board as the opponent faces it.

The words *Queenside* and *Kingside,* like the thick vertical dividing line, are printed on Diagram 1 only for instructional purposes. The side of the board on which the Queens begin the game is called the Queenside, and the side of the board on which the Kings begin the game is called the Kingside. This division of the board—the Queenside on White's left and on Black's right, etc.—does not change, even if later in the game the Queens move to the Kingside and the Kings to the Queenside. Rooks, Knights and Bishops are also labeled Queen Rook, King Rook, Queen Bishop, King Bishop, etc. depending on which side they begin the game.

(When discussing a game, chessplayers find designations such as "King's Knight" are useful mostly during the early stages of a contest, when it is still possible to remember where the piece started the game.)

The lower half of the board is called the **White side** or White territory; the upper half is called the **Black side** or Black territory.

Introducing the terms that are used to describe a chessboard is exciting for no one—teacher or student. The good news is that there is relatively little jargon in chess, and most of the terms are part of common language and self-evident.

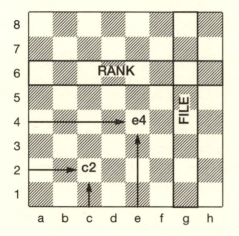

DIAGRAM 2

In Diagram 2, just as in a formation of soldiers, the horizontal rows are called **ranks** and the vertical columns are called **files**. The mysterious numbers running up the left side of the board and the letters slithering across the bottom comprise a grid system that you can use to identify squares and, of course, ranks and files. Ranks are identified by number (the highlighted example is "the sixth rank") and files by letter (the highlighted example is the "g-file").

Identifying squares is elementary: To identify any given square, glance down to find out the file and then glance left to find out the rank. For example, in Diagram 2 the square at the intersection of file "c" and rank "2" is "c2"; the square "e4" is at the intersection of file "e" and rank "4."

Quick, which piece starts out on the g-file? That's right: the Knight. And on which file does the Queen begin its career? You got it: the d-file.

The following chart shows the forces with which White and Black start a game, along with the symbols used to represent chessmen:

NAME	WHITE	BLACK	SYMBOLS
King	1	1	K or ♔ ♚
Queen	1	1	Q or ♕ ♛
Rook	2	2	R or ♖ ♜
Bishop	2	2	B or ♗ ♝
Knight	2	2	N or ♘ ♞
pawn	8	8	P or ♙ ♟

The word *move* means the transfer of a man from its current square to another square. Each player moves in turn, with White starting out the game. No player can skip his turn to move, and no player can make two consecutive moves.

Capturing an opponent's man (captures of your own men are illegal) means removing the man from the board and placing your man onto the same square occupied by the captured enemy man. Unlike checkers, a chessman does not capture by hopping over another man; also unlike checkers, captures are strictly optional, except when necessary to relieve an attack on the King or when no other legal move is possible. Two men cannot simultaneously occupy the same square, which means in turn that one man per square is the maximum.

A captured man—pawn or piece—cannot re-enter the game, which means that the number of men in a game of chess can only decrease, never increase.

HOW THE PIECES AND PAWNS MOVE AND CAPTURE

Each type of chessman has its own way of moving, and all men of the same type—White or Black—move in the same way. What follows is an explanation of the powers provided to each type of man.

The Bishop: The Bishop always moves diagonally along squares of the same color and, like all pieces, may move in any direction, backward or forward. Diagram 3 shows how the Bishop moves in straight lines and cannot change directions during an individual move by breaking this line. In short, no zigzags during a single move.

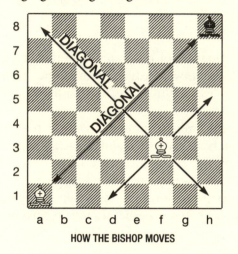

DIAGRAM 3

HOW THE BISHOP MOVES

Each player starts with two Bishops, one on light squares, the other on dark squares. Since the Bishop moves only diagonally, a Bishop that starts out on a light square can never move to a dark one and vice-versa. The Bishop confined to light squares is called the light-squared Bishop, and the one on dark squares, the dark-squared Bishop.

Like all other chessmen, the Bishop captures by placing itself on the square of the targeted enemy man. In Diagram 3, the dark-squared Black Bishop can capture the dark-squared White Bishop by placing itself on the a1-square occupied by that Bishop (and if White instead moved first, he could capture the Black Bishop). On the other hand, the dark-squared Black Bishop cannot under any circumstances capture the light-squared White Bishop and vice-versa. Indeed, since the Bishop can move only on squares of one color, it cannot attack any enemy man on a square of the other color.

A Bishop can move to any vacant square of the same color on which it stands; however, it cannot hop over—that is, move through—men of either color blocking the way.

The approximate value of a Bishop is 3 points on a scale where a pawn counts as 1 point. On the edge of the board, a Bishop controls seven squares; in the center, it controls a maximum of 13 squares.

The Rook: The Rook (also known as the *Castle*) can move to any vacant square on the rank or file on which it stands, provided that no men of either color block the path.

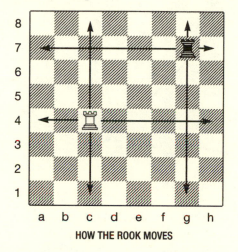

DIAGRAM 4

HOW THE ROOK MOVES

Like all other chess men, the Rook captures an enemy man by removing it from the board and occupying the square where it stood. The Rook is obviously highly mobile and can go from one end or one side of the board to the other, but like the Bishop, it can travel only in a straight line on any given move. No zigzagging.

No matter where a Rook is placed on an empty board, it controls 14 squares and has a value of 5 points, compared to 3 for the Bishop.

The Queen: The Queen is the most powerful piece in chess, and from any square in the center controls 27 squares. From the corners, it controls 21 squares—its smallest number on an open board.

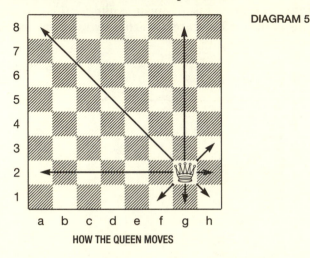

DIAGRAM 5

HOW THE QUEEN MOVES

Diagram 5 shows how the Queen combines the powers of the Bishop and Rook. On an open board, it can move in any direction along the entire length of any rank, file, or diagonal on which it stands. Like the Bishop and Rook, it captures an enemy piece by removing it from the board and assuming the square on which the fallen enemy stood. Also like the Bishop and Rook, the Queen cannot move through friendly or enemy pieces and must proceed in a straight line on any given move. No zigzagging.

The Queen is valued at 9 points (or approximately Rook + Bishop + pawn), and its power is illustrated in the following diagram, where this tough-as-nails chess career woman can wipe out any of eight enemy men:

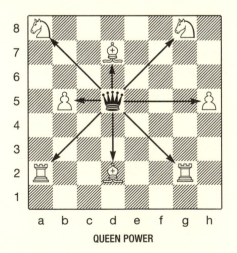

DIAGRAM 6

QUEEN POWER

The Knight: The Knight (also sometimes called a ***Horse***) moves in an L-shaped pattern:

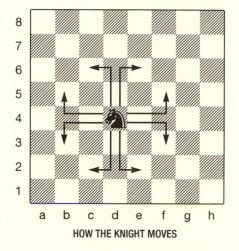

DIAGRAM 7

HOW THE KNIGHT MOVES

One-two-and-over, one-two-and-over; the Knight prances with a jaunty dance step. Like the Bishop, Rook and Queen, the Knight captures an enemy man by removing it from the board and assuming the square it occupied. But unlike these other pieces, it obviously does not move in a straight line and is the only chess piece that can jump over other men—either its own or the opponent's. The Knight cannot capture any of the pieces that it leaps over, only an enemy piece on the destination square.

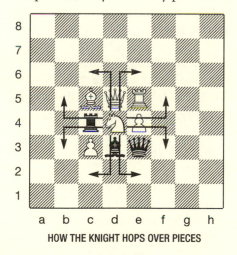

DIAGRAM 8

HOW THE KNIGHT HOPS OVER PIECES

From a post in the center or on the ranks and files immediately adjacent to the center, the Knight can control eight squares, compared with 14 for the Rooks. To traverse the chessboard from one side to the other requires four moves compared to one for the Bishop, Rook and Queen on an open board. Further, the Knight loses power radically in the corners where it controls only two squares and along the edges where its maximum count is four squares.

The Knight's value is 3 points, which makes it approximately equal to a Bishop. All things being equal, advanced players prefer Bishops over Knights. Among beginners and other less experienced players, however, the non-linear movements of the Knight create confusion and make it at least the equal of a Bishop in practical play. You need only look at Diagram 8 to realize that a Knight can simultaneously attack up to eight enemy men. In many games it lands up forking two or more enemy men, which means that it attacks these men simultaneously.

And here is another unusual power of the Knight:

DIAGRAM 9

SMOTHERED MATE

Keeping in mind the earlier definition of checkmate, which is an attack on the King that cannot be parried, you can see that Black's Knight has checkmated the White King, which is literally smothered by its own pieces. Hence the term *smothered mate*—a kind of checkmate that we analyze in Chapter 7.

The Pawn: Pawns are the foot soldiers of chess and would be anonymous in their sameness were they not individually identified as the Queen pawn, the King pawn and so on, according to the piece standing behind their respective starting positions.

Pawns may advance forward toward the enemy side, but unlike pieces, they can never retreat. No R & R back in the rear lines for these guys. They move forward one square at a time along the file on which they stand.

Each pawn, no matter how far the game has progressed, has the option on its first move (and only on its first move) of moving forward either one or two squares.

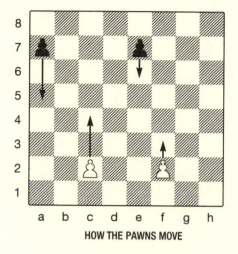

DIAGRAM 10

HOW THE PAWNS MOVE

If an enemy or friendly man is on the square straight in front of a pawn, the pawn can neither advance nor capture the roadblock. In Diagram 11, none of the pawns can capture one another and are, therefore, stuck.

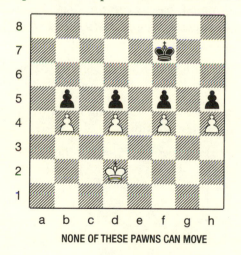

DIAGRAM 11

NONE OF THESE PAWNS CAN MOVE

Although a pawn moves straight ahead, it can capture only to the side—that is, one square diagonally forward. It cannot capture backward. In Diagram 12, White's Queenside pawn can capture the Knight but not the pawn directly in front of it, while White's Kingside pawn can capture either Black's pawn or Queen. As for Black's pawns, the one on d7 can capture either the White Bishop or Rook, while the one on e3 can rub out its fellow pawn.

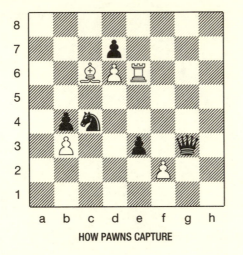

DIAGRAM 12

HOW PAWNS CAPTURE

As with the pieces already discussed, the pawn removes the captured enemy and occupies the latter's square.

As noted, the first time each pawn moves, it has the option of advancing one or two squares; as noted, pawns capture diagonally one square forward. Which brings us to a special type of pawn capture.

En passant captures occur when:

· White has a pawn on the fifth rank (as in Diagram 13) or Black has a pawn on the fourth rank.

· An enemy pawn on an immediately adjoining file moves forward two squares from its initial starting position.

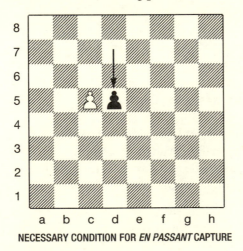

DIAGRAM 13

NECESSARY CONDITION FOR *EN PASSANT* CAPTURE

White may now capture and remove Black's pawn as if it had advanced only one square as shown in Diagram 14:

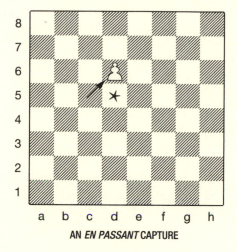

DIAGRAM 14

AN *EN PASSANT* CAPTURE

The option to capture *en passant* must be exercised by the capturing side on its very first move following the two-square advance of the opponent's pawn. If a move intervenes, the enemy pawn is safe from *en passant* capture for the remainder of the game. *En passant* does not extend to pieces; it is strictly a private matter between pawns.

As with all other captures by pieces and pawns, *en passant* is compulsory only when it is the only legal move available—for example, when it is the single way to remove a King from attack.

Here is a list of the four necessary conditions for an *en passant* capture to be legal:

1. If the pawn is White and doing the capturing, it must be on the fifth rank; if Black, on the fourth rank.

2. The pawn doing the capturing and the pawn being captured must be on adjacent files.

3. The pawn to be captured must have advanced two squares in a single move from its initial starting position.

4. The pawn doing the capturing must exercise the option on the very next turn and capture diagonally forward as if the enemy pawn had advanced only one square.

If a pawn reaches the other end of the board, it must be **promoted** to any piece of its own color—Bishop, Rook, Queen, or Knight, but not a King. The pawn is the only man that can be promoted; pieces do not possess this capability. The actual mechanics of pawn promotion involve removing the pawn from the promotion or Queening square and replacing it with a piece of one's choice.

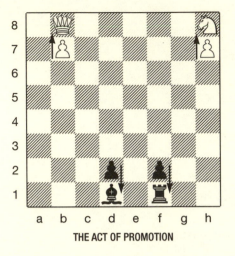

DIAGRAM 15

THE ACT OF PROMOTION

Can a player have two or three Queens, Rooks, Bishops, or Knights? Absolutely. Under the rules of chess, a player may have up to nine Queens on the board or 10 Rooks and so on. Promoting a pawn and replacing it with the desired piece counts as one move, and the new piece has exactly the same powers as a "natural-born" one. Of course, if a pawn reaches the other end of the board by capturing an enemy piece, then that piece is also removed from the board.

The King: As the most important piece on the board, the King has been called "the heart and sole" of chess. Lose a Queen, and you can keep playing; lose your King to checkmate, and the game is over. On the spot.

The actual fighting power of the King is limited to a maximum of eight squares, with the monarch moving one square in any direction.

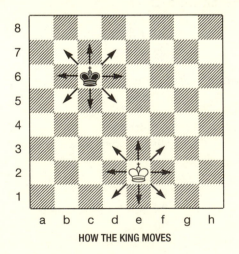

DIAGRAM 16

HOW THE KING MOVES

The King captures the same way as it moves, and like all of the other pieces, it removes the man taken and occupies the latter's square. But there is one difference: While other pieces can capture an opponent's man even though it is protected by another member of the enemy's force, a King cannot do so. In this situation, for example, the White King cannot capture the Black Knight ...

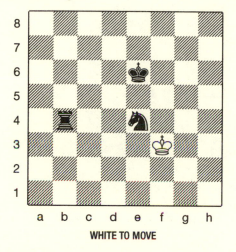

DIAGRAM 17

WHITE TO MOVE

... because making such a capture means moving the King into...

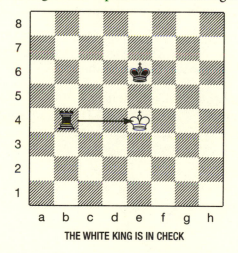

DIAGRAM 18

THE WHITE KING IS IN CHECK

... check! Which is illegal. A *check* occurs when the King is attacked by an enemy man, and a King that is "in check" must immediately escape it. If the King cannot escape check, then it is in checkmate; the game is over.

Here are four examples of chess men delivering check, with the bold arrow indicating the move that delivers the check and the light arrow showing the actual check or attack on the King.

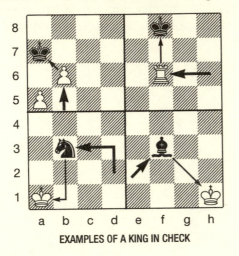

DIAGRAM 19

EXAMPLES OF A KING IN CHECK

Earlier we listed the three requirements for checkmate, which are the mirror image of the three methods for escaping check. To escape check, a King can:

1. Move to a safe square not attacked by the enemy.

2. Interpose one of his own men between the enemy and himself.

3. Capture the enemy piece that is delivering the check.

If he can do none of these things, he is in mate.

Checking *per se* is neither good nor bad. The features of a specific position determine whether the check is worthwhile or an overdraft. Many beginners try to check whenever possible. "Always check, it might be mate!" is their motto.

Don't let that be your motto. Remember: Checking is strictly optional, and like all other options in chess it should be carefully considered.

If the King cannot escape check, then he is in *checkmate:*

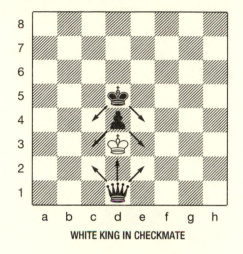

DIAGRAM 20

WHITE KING IN CHECKMATE

In Diagram 20, the Black Queen threatens to capture the King, which is too far away to capture the Queen. The King has no piece to interpose between himself and the enemy Queen and no piece to capture the Queen. The King also cannot flee to a free square; all such squares are covered by the enemy King, Queen and pawn as indicated by the arrows. Finally, the White King cannot capture the pawn because it would be subject to capture in return by Black's King or Queen.

Is the Black King in checkmate in Diagram 21?

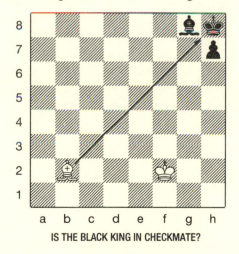

DIAGRAM 21

IS THE BLACK KING IN CHECKMATE?

Yes. Ask yourself the following questions when deciding if the Black monarch can escape the check by White's Bishop:

1. Can the Black King move? No, it is blocked by its own men.

2. Can the check be blocked? No, Black's Bishop and pawn cannot go to a dark square to block the White Bishop.

3. Can the White Bishop be captured? No.

A KING'S HOME IS HIS CASTLE

Along with *en passant* captures for pawns, there is a second special move in chess that involves a King and Rook. It is called *castling* and counts as one move even though the King and Rook move simultaneously. In castling, the King can cooperate with either the Queen Rook or the King Rook.

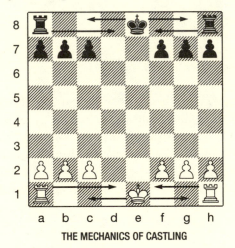

DIAGRAM 22

THE MECHANICS OF CASTLING

The mechanics of castling require that the King move two squares toward the intended Rook, which is then placed on the first square that the King crossed. In Diagram 22, the arrows show the paths and destinations of the King and the Rooks for both Kingside and Queenside castling. Notice that when castling takes place on the Kingside, the Rook moves two squares; on the Queenside, three squares.

Diagram 23 shows the completed process when White castles Kingside and Black on the Queenside. Compare the positions of King and Rook with the arrows in Diagram 22.

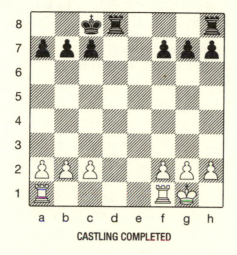

DIAGRAM 23

CASTLING COMPLETED

Castling should be played as soon as possible during a game because it tucks the King in a secure corner far away from attacks in the center, while also bringing a Rook into action.

A player may castle only once in a game in accord with these rules:

1. Castling is forbidden if either the King or the Rook that is intended to be used has already moved at any point in the game.

2. All the squares between the King and Rook must be empty. Neither piece can jump over or capture other pieces while castling.

3. The King cannot castle to get out of check. However, if a King escapes check without itself moving, it may later castle when no longer in check.

4. The King cannot move into or through check when castling, which means that a King cannot land up on a square where he is in check and cannot pass through squares controlled by enemy men.

On the other hand, castling is permitted if the intended Rook is under attack or if the Rook passes through a square (either b1 or b8) attacked, though not occupied, by an opponent's man.

THE CONCEPT OF WINNING MATERIAL

When explaining how pieces and pawns move, we provided the point value of each man, which is a relative measure of its capacity to control squares compared with the other men. The following table is a review:

PIECE	VALUE
Queen	9
Rook	5
Bishop	3
Knight	3
pawn	1

Some chess players will argue that a Bishop should be valued at $3\frac{1}{2}$ points. All things being equal, most advanced chess players prefer a Bishop (for its long range) over a Knight (which moves in little hops). But all things are rarely equal in a chess game, and sometimes the Bishop's limited scope (it can move on squares of only one color) give it a distinct disadvantage against a Knight. For the purpose of evaluating the relative strength of the men, we value both the Bishop and Knight at 3 points for beginning and intermediate players. In any particular situation, you may find that either piece is slightly more valuable than the other.

As for the King, its value lies primarily in staying out of harm's way. At the beginning and in the middle of the game, the King is exceedingly weak and must avoid churning action lest it get mated. In the final phase of the game, when there are reduced attacking forces, the King often enters the game as a fighting piece, when its strength is about 3 points, which makes it approximately equal to a Knight.

Winning material means picking off pieces and pawns of the opponent that are left unprotected or making advantageous trades, such as surrendering, say, a Bishop for a Rook or giving up a Bishop and Knight (6 points) for a Queen (9 points). Although the object of chess is not to win material but to checkmate the opponent's King, the side that gains a preponderance of material often delivers checkmate because of the extra pawns and pieces.

Bobby Fischer has said that unless one sees a concrete reason not to capture a piece or a pawn advantageously, then do it. Winning material usually leaves the opponent less able to resist attacks or to mount counterattacks, which means that you are more likely to win.

HOW GAMES ARE DRAWN

Since chess games are won by delivering checkmate, if neither side can do so, then a game is drawn. King versus King is, for example, a draw by force, since the rules prevent either monarch from approaching the other because such an approach entails moving into check.

The most common reason for a draw is that one player offers a draw, and the other accepts. Often the two players see little purpose in playing further because the game is very even. Or, perhaps, one player offers a draw knowing that he stands worse, but the opponent accepts because he mistakenly believes the position to be even.

Another kind of draw is called *stalemate*, which occurs when one side has no legal move. The game is then a draw even if the other side has a huge advantage in every sector. In Diagram 24, it is White's turn to move. Black is up a Rook and pawn, but the game is drawn because White has no legal move.

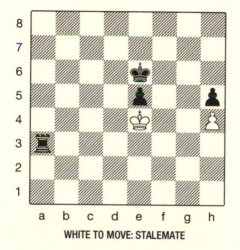

DIAGRAM 24

WHITE TO MOVE: STALEMATE

White's pawn is blocked by Black's Rook pawn and cannot move. The White King is not in check, yet it cannot move because all possible squares are guarded by Black's King, Rook and pawn. Notice how the Rook sweeps across the third rank and how the King and pawn deprive the White King of possible squares. White is clearly in stalemate because he can make no legal move with his King or with any other piece.

Another kind of draw is by a *three-fold repetition* of position. A player can claim a draw if the move he is about to make will repeat the same position for a third time. He may wish to do so because he is otherwise losing and wishes to take advantage of the three-fold repetition rule.

A fourth species of draw is by *perpetual check,* a three-fold repetition of position that occurs when one side can check (though not checkmate) the other side so that the same position occurs three times.

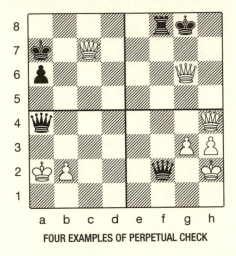

DIAGRAM 25

FOUR EXAMPLES OF PERPETUAL CHECK

Examine the position in the upper-right corner of Diagram 25. The White Queen can check the Black King back and forth in the corner, though it cannot deliver mate. White's motive in forcing a draw by three-fold repetition of position could be that Black was winning elsewhere on the board, and perpetual check offered the only chance to draw.

When 50 moves—meaning 50 pairs of moves, one by each side—go by with no capture or pawn move being made, then either player can claim a draw. A player with a King and Rook against a King must, for example, checkmate within 50 moves.

Finally, a player can claim a draw if no mating material remains on the board. A King-versus-King ending is drawn, since neither side can deliver checkmate. For the same reason, so are endings of King + Bishop versus King, King + Knight versus King, and King + Bishop versus King + Bishop if the two Bishops move on squares of the same color. Several of these endings are discussed at greater length in Chapter 9.

You are now ready to play your first game of chess.

CHESS MOVIE: BAD DAY AT BLACK ROCK

Congratulations in advance! You are about to play and win your first game of chess—with a bit of help from the brilliant nineteenth-century German wizard, Johann Zukertort. You have White with Zukertort, and your opponent is Adolf Anderssen, whom some chess writers regard as world champion from 1851 to 1858 and from 1862 to 1866, even though an official world title did not exist until 1886. The scene is Breslau, when this city was part of the German Empire; the year is 1865. And you are in luck: Anderssen is about to have a spectacularly bad day with Black.

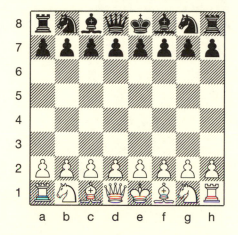

DIAGRAM 26

1. Set up your chessboard as shown in Diagram 1. Be careful. Have you placed a White square in the right-hand corner? Is the White Queen on a light square, and the Black Queen on a dark square? You are playing White and make the first move.

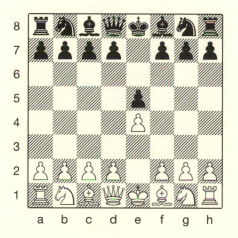

DIAGRAM 27

2. Move the pawn in front of the White King forward two squares. Then do the same thing for the pawn in front of the Black King to reach the above position. Notice how both pawns now occupy two of the four squares in the center of the board. Control of the center is crucial.

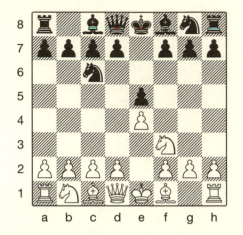

DIAGRAM 28

3. Move the White Knight on the Kingside of the board to the light square shown above; move the Black Knight on the Queenside of the board to the light square shown above. The Knight makes L-shaped moves and can jump over pieces of either side. The White King Knight attacks Black's King pawn, and Black defends the pawn with his Queen Knight.

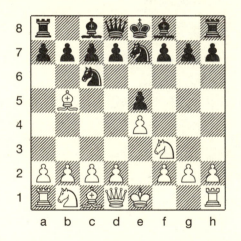

DIAGRAM 29

4. The White Bishop next to the King slides forward to the light square four ranks in front of White's Queen Knight, and Black's King Knight occupies the dark square directly in front of its King. Both sides are playing an ancient, though still popular, opening called the Ruy Lopez.

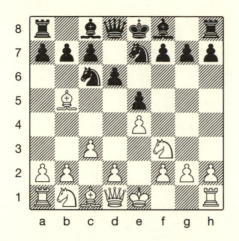

DIAGRAM 30

5. Push the pawn in front of White's Queen Bishop forward one square, and do likewise for the pawn in front of Black's Queen. White has just moved a pawn that keeps an "eye" on the diagonal dark square in the center. In chess, most strategic roads lead to the center.

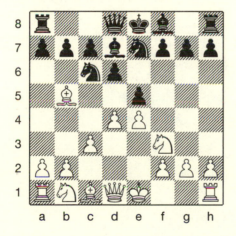

DIAGRAM 31

6. Talk about central control! White pushes the pawn in front of his Queen forward two squares, with the idea of pushing it one square further, where it will threaten to capture the Black Knight. Black responds by moving a Bishop directly in front of his Queen.

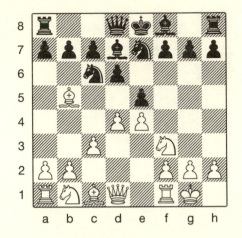

DIAGRAM 32

7. White castles—as described on page 28. Notice that White moves his King two squares to the right and brings his Rook directly to the King's left. Part of White's strategy has been to quickly move both his King Knight and King Bishop so that his King could find safety by castling.

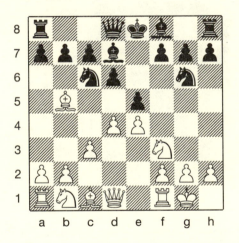

DIAGRAM 33

8. Black moves the Knight in front of his King to the light square as shown above. Unlike White's King, the Black monarch remains on a central file, where it can be attacked. In only six more moves, you and your colleague, Johann Zukertort, will checkmate the great Adolf Anderssen.

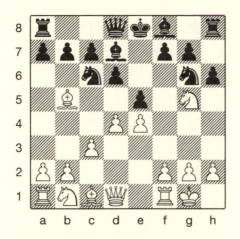

DIAGRAM 34

9. White moves forward the King Knight to the dark square shown above, pressing the attack. Black responds by moving the pawn in front of the Kingside Rook one square, threatening to capture the Knight. Must the more valuable White Knight retreat?

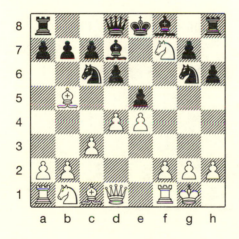

DIAGRAM 35

10. No! White delivers a chessic uppercut by capturing the pawn on the light square next to Black's King. Remove this pawn from the board and put the White Knight in its place. This Knight can now be captured by the Black King, which in the process loses his protective covering.

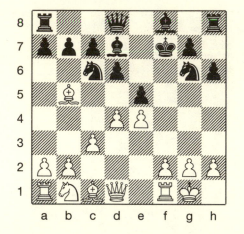

DIAGRAM 36

11. Black captures the White Knight by removing it from the board and putting his King on the square. In terms of fighting units, Black has gained a Knight (3 points) in exchange for a pawn (1 point). Normally a good trade. But here White can vigorously attack the King.

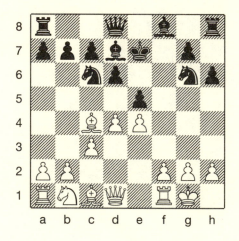

DIAGRAM 37

12. Move White's light-squared Bishop to the square shown above, where it delivers check (see page 25) on the Black King by threatening to capture it. Black sidesteps the threat of capture by shuffling his King to the dark square shown above. Black soon finds that while he can run, he can't hide.

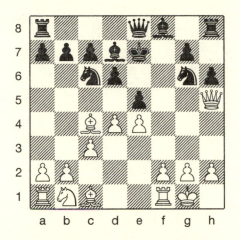

DIAGRAM 38

13. White slides his powerful Queen along the light squares to the position shown above, threatening to capture the adjacent Black Knight, which Black quickly guards by playing his Queen to the King's original square. White attacks, Black defends. With Black a piece to the good and with White on the offensive, the position seems in balance ...

DIAGRAM 39

14. ... but only for a moment! White slides his Queen one square to the left, placing the Black King in check, thereby threatening to capture it and win the game. Black cannot interpose a piece and cannot move his King to the light squares commanded by White's Bishop. Hey, wait one second!

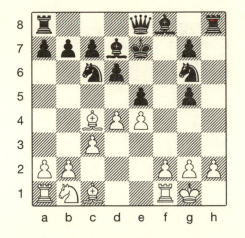

DIAGRAM 40

15. Can't Black's lowly King Rook pawn capture the White Queen? Yes, by removing the White Queen and putting the pawn in its place as shown above. So far, White has lost his Knight and Queen (9 points), but he has gained a ...

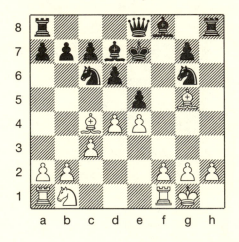

DIAGRAM 41

16. King! Simply move White's dark-squared Bishop to capture the pawn that just took the Queen. Black's King is in checkmate (see page 27)! Anderssen's King cannot escape capture by one of White's two Bishops. Black can neither capture the Bishop attacking his King nor interpose a piece.

2 *Chessercizes: All the Right Moves*

IN CHAPTER 1 YOU LEARNED every rule necessary to play a legal game of chess. You learned about such concepts as check, checkmate, drawn games, and the relative value of the pieces. Now it's time to stretch your mental muscles by practicing what you've learned. Examine each diagram and then answer the questions to the side of the diagram. The answers are at the bottom of the page. If your answer is wrong or, still worse, if you fail to understand why it is wrong, then review the relevant portion of Chapter 1.

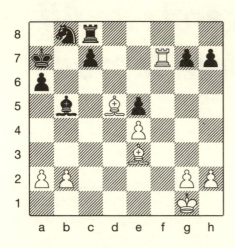

DIAGRAM 42

1. Is Black in checkmate?

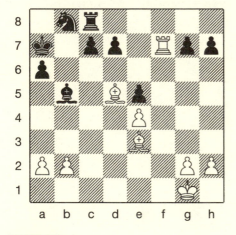

DIAGRAM 43

2. Is Black in checkmate?

ANSWERS

1. Yes. The dark-squared White Bishop threatens to capture the Black King, and Black has no way to avoid this capture. The Black King cannot go to a light square because of White's other Bishop bearing down.

2. No. The position here is identical to Chessercize No. 1, except that Black has a pawn on d7, and Black can now move the pawn in front of his Rook two squares to relieve the check. In Chessercize No. 1, this pawn move would illegally put the Black King in check from the White Rook.

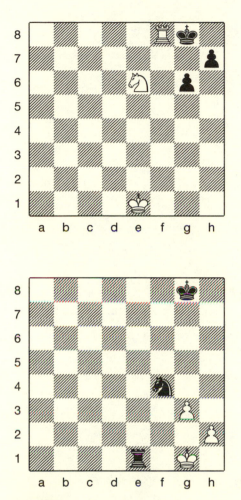

DIAGRAM 44

3. Is Black in checkmate?

DIAGRAM 45

4. Is White in checkmate?

ANSWERS

3. Yes. Notice how the Knight guards both the Rook and the possible escape square directly in front of the Black King.

4. No. White's King can escape check by moving diagonally to the adjacent dark square.

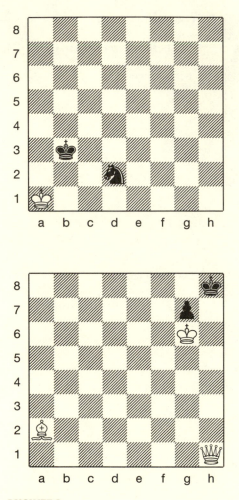

DIAGRAM 46

5. Is White in checkmate?

DIAGRAM 47

6. Is Black in checkmate?

ANSWERS

5. No. Look closely. White is not even in check! Instead, the game is a draw by stalemate (see page 31). Remember: King + Knight cannot checkmate a lone King. The same goes for King + Bishop versus a lone King.

6. Yes. Did you notice that the Bishop out in left field controls the light square next to Black's King?

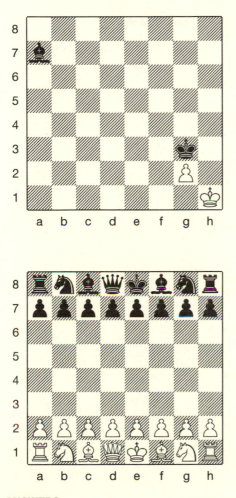

DIAGRAM 48

7. Is White in checkmate?

DIAGRAM 49

8. Is everything set up correctly to begin play?

ANSWERS

7. No. It is a draw by stalemate.

8. No. The board is set up incorrectly with a dark square in the lower right-hand corner (see page 13). Notice that the Kings and Queens of both sides are on the wrong-colored squares for starting the game.

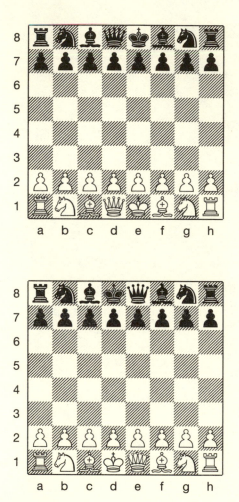

DIAGRAM 50

9. What is wrong with this setup?

DIAGRAM 51

10. Are White and Black ready to play?

ANSWERS

9. Nothing at all. You are ready to start playing.

10. No. Both sides need to switch their Kings and Queens. Remember the rule: The White Queen begins on a light square; the Black Queen starts on a dark square. White Queen on white, Black Queen on black.

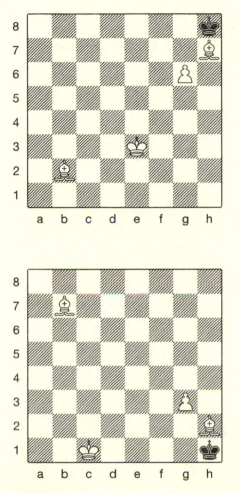

DIAGRAM 52

11. Is Black in checkmate?

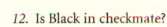

DIAGRAM 53

12. Is Black in checkmate?

ANSWERS

11. Yes. The Black King has no escape and cannot take the Bishop because the pawn guards it.

12. No. Black can capture the dark-squared Bishop because pawns cannot move or capture backwards.

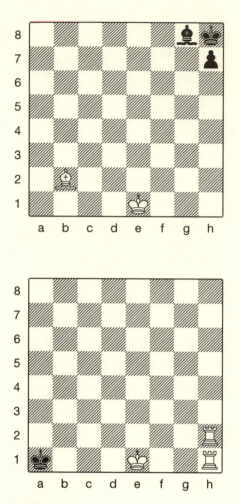

DIAGRAM 54

13. Is Black in checkmate?

DIAGRAM 55

14. Can White checkmate Black in one move?

ANSWERS

13. Yes. The Black King is hemmed in by its own pieces (see Diagram 21 on page 27).

14. Yes. White simply castles.

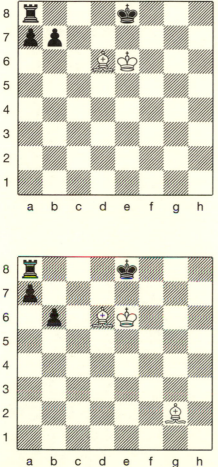

DIAGRAM 56

15. Can Black castle legally?

DIAGRAM 57

16. Can Black castle legally?

ANSWERS

15. Yes. It makes no difference if the Rook passes through territory controlled by the Bishop (see page 29).

16. Yes. It makes no difference if the Rook is under attack (see page 29).

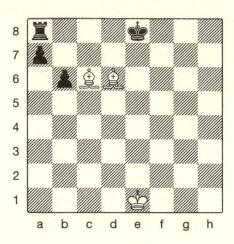

DIAGRAM 58

17. Can Black castle legally?

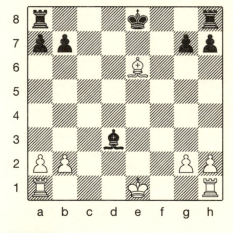

DIAGRAM 59

18. On which side of the board can White castle legally? On which side of the board can Black castle legally?

ANSWERS

17. No. The Black King is in check, and it is illegal to castle out of check (see page 29).

18. White can castle legally on the Queenside but not on the Kingside because his King must travel through check on the light square immediately to the right. Black cannot castle legally on either side because in each instance his King finishes in check on a light square controlled by White's Bishop.

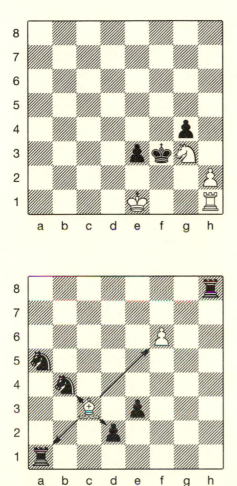

DIAGRAM 60

19. How can White checkmate in one move?

DIAGRAM 61

20. Which pieces cannot be captured by the White Bishop?

ANSWERS

19. White simply castles. The Black King cannot escape to either of the light squares diagonally to his right because they are controlled by the White Knight.

20. The White Bishop cannot capture its own pawn or any of the Black pieces that are without the pointing arrows because it cannot move over pieces (see page 16).

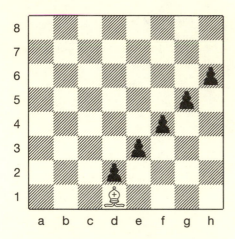

DIAGRAM 62

21. Can any of the Black pawns advance to White's back row and promote to a Queen?

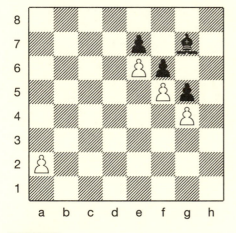

DIAGRAM 63

22. Can the Black Bishop stop the White pawn on the Queenside from advancing to make a Queen?

ANSWERS

21. No. If a Black pawn moves forward to a light square, it will be subject to capture by the Bishop.

22. No. The Bishop is hemmed in by his own pawns, which are themselves unable to move. Remember: Pawns move straight ahead but can only capture diagonally (see page 21).

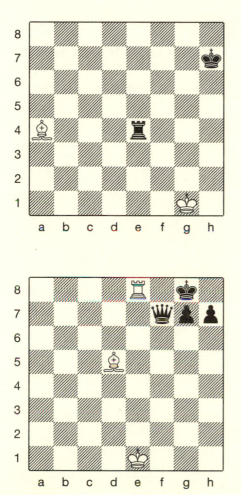

DIAGRAM 64

23. Can White win the Black Rook?

DIAGRAM 65

24. Why is this position won for White?

ANSWERS

23. Yes. By moving the Bishop backward two squares to c2, White attacks the Rook, which cannot move because the Bishop could then capture the Black King. In chess parlance, the Bishop has put the Rook into a *pin*, which is a tactic that in this instance prevents the Rook from moving because it shields against an attack on the King. A piece is said to be pinned when it is under attack and when its moving would put another of its own men under attack.

24. Black is in checkmate. The Queen cannot capture the Rook because the Bishop would then attack the Black King.

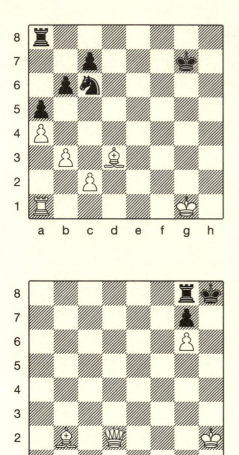

DIAGRAM 66

25. Can White win a piece?

DIAGRAM 67

26. Can White checkmate in one move?

ANSWERS

25. Yes. The Bishop moves one square forward to the right (on e4), attacking the Knight. The Knight is pinned because if it moves, the Bishop captures the Rook.

26. Yes. Move the Queen diagonally until it is two squares in front of the Black King at h6. The Black pawn cannot capture the Queen because doing so exposes his King to attack by the Bishop.

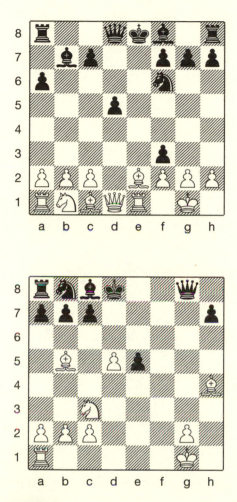

DIAGRAM 68

27. Can White checkmate in one move?

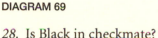

DIAGRAM 69

28. Is Black in checkmate?

ANSWERS

27. Yes. Move White's light-squared Bishop three squares forward to b5. Notice that the Black King is now in ***double check*** by both the Bishop and White's Rook next to his Queen. In such a situation, forget about trying to move a piece in front of the threatened King. When in double check, the King must move. In this case it has no place to go and is, therefore, in checkmate.

28. No, not yet. Black can interpose his Queen directly in front of White's dark-squared Bishop, though White can capture the Queen, and Black is then in checkmate. Notice how the crisscross action of White's Bishops controls all of the escape squares of Black's King.

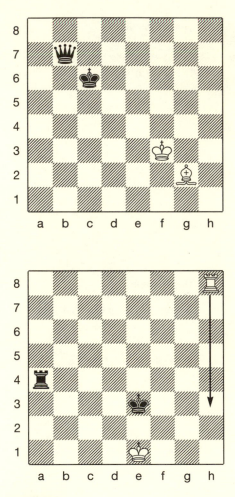

DIAGRAM 70

29. Can White make a draw?

DIAGRAM 71

30. Why does White win the Black Rook by checking on the indicated square? What happens if it is Black's turn to move in the above position?

ANSWERS

29. Black has a Queen against White's Bishop, which should be enough to win. But White can uncover his Bishop with check on the Black King by moving his King to any dark square or to any of the light squares except for the one (e4) in front of the Bishop. When the Black King moves, White captures the Queen, and the Black King takes the Bishop. King versus King is a draw.

30. After White checks on the indicated square, Black's King must move backward because it cannot go forward into squares controlled by White's King. The White Rook can then check on the dark square (h4) immediately in front of the indicated square, and when Black again moves his King, White captures the Black Rook. If Black moves first, he immediately checkmates White by moving his Rook three squares forward to the corner dark square of a1.

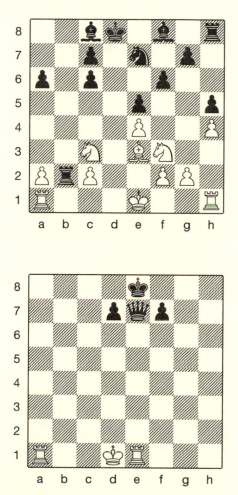

DIAGRAM 72

31. On which side should White castle?

DIAGRAM 73

32. How can White checkmate in one move?

ANSWERS

31. White can castle legally on either side. But the winning move is castling on the Queenside, simultaneously checking the Black King and threatening to capture the Black Rook on b2.

32. Push the Rook on the left of White's King to a8 at the other end of the board. Black is in checkmate because the Queen is pinned by White's other Rook.

DIAGRAM 74

33. How does White checkmate in two moves?

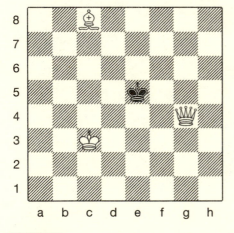

DIAGRAM 75

34. How does White checkmate in one move?

ANSWERS

33. White checkmates in two moves by sliding the King Rook directly to the right of his King, putting the Black King in check. Black must play his Queen directly in front of his King. White now checkmates with the identical move, as in Chessercize 32.

34. White slides his Queen to the dark square of d4 between the two Kings. Black is in checkmate! The diagonal power of the Queen and Bishop is quite striking.

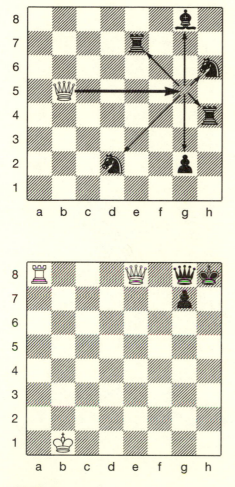

DIAGRAM 76

35. What happens when the White Queen moves to the indicated square?

DIAGRAM 77

36. Point out the two checkmates that White can play.

ANSWERS

35. On the indicated square, White's Queen simultaneously attacks all six of Black's men. A good example of why the Queen has the highest fighting value of all the pieces.

36. White can checkmate by capturing the Black Queen or by moving his Queen to h5, three squares in front of Black's King.

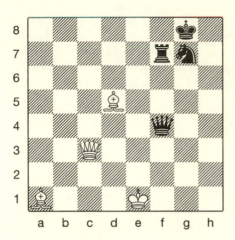

DIAGRAM 78

37. How does White checkmate in one move?

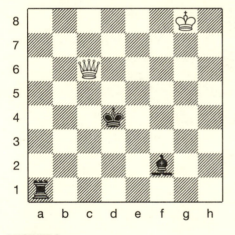

DIAGRAM 79

38. How does White force the win of the Black Rook?

ANSWERS

37. White checkmates by capturing the Knight with his Queen. Notice that the Black Rook cannot move because White's light-squared Bishop could then capture the enemy King.

38. White wins the Rook by moving his Queen three squares to the right at f6, where it checks the Black King on the dark-square diagonal. When the Black King moves, it exposes the Rook to capture. A *skewer* is a tactic in which an opponent's piece is forced to move off the line of attack, exposing another man to capture or allowing the opponent to occupy a key square. In this example, White has skewered Black's Rook.

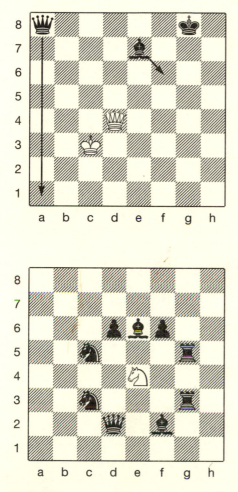

DIAGRAM 80

39. How does moving the Bishop to the indicated square win the White Queen?

DIAGRAM 81

40. Which piece can the White Knight not capture?

ANSWERS

39. White must capture the Bishop that moves to the square indicated by the arrow. Whereupon, Black zooms his Queen directly ahead to the dark square of a1 at the other end of the board, when he skewers the White King and Queen.

40. White cannot capture the light-squared Bishop.

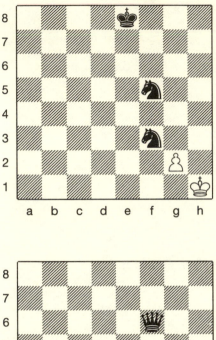

DIAGRAM 82

41. How does Black checkmate in one move?

DIAGRAM 83

42. How can White force a draw?

ANSWERS

41. Move the Knight to g3, where it can check the White King. It is also checkmate.

42. The Knight can fork Black's King and Queen by moving three squares in front of the White King to e4. Although White will then be ahead a Knight, the game is drawn because King + Knight cannot checkmate a lone King. Do not forget that King + Bishop also cannot checkmate a lone King. A *fork* occurs when a Knight or pawn attacks at least two enemy units on the same move.

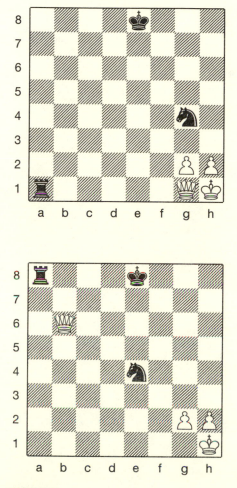

DIAGRAM 84

43. How does Black checkmate in one move?

DIAGRAM 85

44. How does Black checkmate in two moves?

ANSWERS

43. Move the Knight to f2, which is adjacent to the White Queen, and White is checkmated. The Black Rook pins the Queen to the King, thus preventing the Queen from capturing the Knight.

44. Black mates with a Rook check (the Queen moves next to the White King), and Black then delivers the same mate as in Chessercize 43.

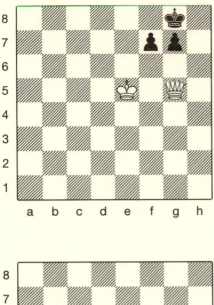

DIAGRAM 86

45. Can Black move and force a draw?

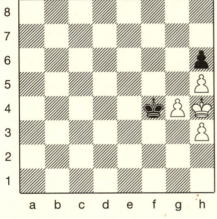

DIAGRAM 87

46. With White to move, who is winning?

ANSWERS

45. Yes. Black moves his light-squared pawn one space, forking the King and Queen. The Queen captures this pawn, whereupon Black captures the Queen and checks the King with his remaining pawn. White then captures this pawn. The result is a King-versus-King draw.

46. Black is winning! White has only one legal move, advancing the pawn that stands between the two Kings. Black captures the pawn with his single remaining pawn, delivering checkmate. In both chess and life, every pawn has his day.

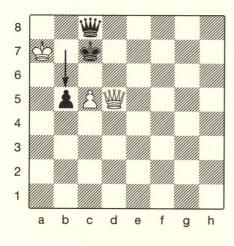

DIAGRAM 88

47. Black has just moved his pawn two squares as indicated by the arrow. How can White checkmate in one move?

DIAGRAM 89

48. How does White checkmate in one move?

ANSWERS

47. White checkmates by taking the pawn *en passant*. Check out this rule on page 22.

48. White checkmates by advancing the pawn one square and promoting it to a Knight—one of the rare moments when a Knight is stronger than a Queen!

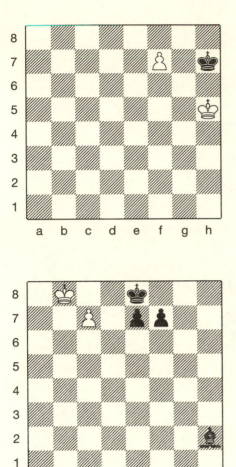

DIAGRAM 90

49. What is White's best move?

DIAGRAM 91

50. Can White advance his pawn and promote it to a King? Can he make a Queen and checkmate Black?

ANSWERS

49. The best move is to advance the pawn one square and promote it (see page 23) to a Rook, when White can eventually checkmate Black. If White promotes the pawn to a Queen, Black's King is in stalemate, and the game is drawn. If he promotes it to a Bishop or Knight, he will lack mating material. See the solution to Chessercize 42.

50. No, it is illegal to promote a pawn to a King (or to let it remain as a pawn). The player promoting a pawn must exchange it for Queen, Rook, Bishop, or Knight. No, White cannot move the pawn forward to make a Queen because Black's Bishop pins it on the King.

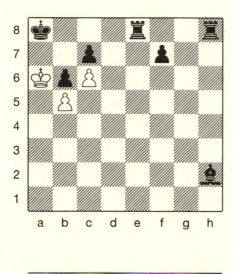

DIAGRAM 92

51. With Black to move, is the
position a draw?

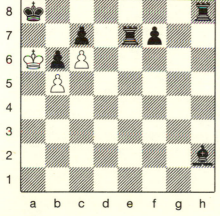

DIAGRAM 93

52. With Black to move, is the
position a draw?

ANSWERS

51. In spite of Black's overwhelming material advantage, the game is a draw. The White King is in stalemate because neither he nor his two pawns can move. Black can do nothing with his coming move to change this situation.

52. Black can avoid a stalemate by sacrificing material in order to give White some legal moves. First, Black moves the Rook on e7 one square over to d7, where the White pawn that is farthest advanced must capture it. Black then pushes forward to c6 the Black pawn adjacent to White's capturing pawn. White's King may now move after his remaining pawn captures the Black pawn on c6. Black will eventually checkmate White because of his vast superiority in material.

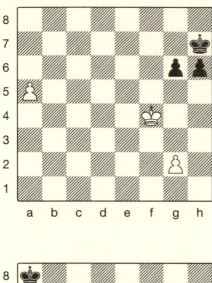

DIAGRAM 94

53. With Black to move, he offered a draw in a position with equal material. Should White accept?

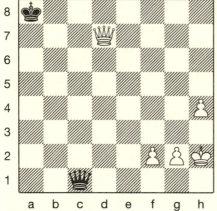

DIAGRAM 95

54. How can Black make a draw?

ANSWERS

53. White should not accept the draw offer. His pawn on the left or Queenside of the board must move only three times to make a Queen, while the Black King must move six times to intercept it. White clearly wins the race. As for Black's two pawns, they are five squares away from Queening—not to mention the fact that White's King is ideally placed to intercept them.

54. Black moves his Queen to the dark square (c7) directly next to White's Queen, checking the White King and virtually forcing the White Queen to capture it. After the capture, the Black King is in stalemate!

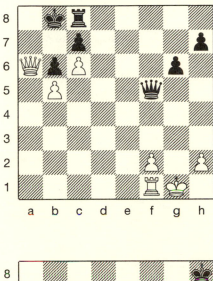

DIAGRAM 96

55. With White threatening to checkmate on b7, can Black move and make a draw?

DIAGRAM 97

56. With White to move, what happens? With Black to move, what happens?

ANSWERS

55. Yes, Black can draw by perpetual check (see page 32), which means delivering a series of checks that the enemy King cannot escape. Black advances his Queen to the light square on its immediate left, checking the White King, which must move into the corner. Black then checks the King again on the light square at f3, directly in front of White's Rook. By moving between these two squares until the same position occurs three times, Black draws through three-fold repetition (see page 31) by using the device of perpetual check.

56. If it is his move, White can checkmate by moving the Queen straight ahead six squares to g7. With Black to move, the game is drawn by stalemate, since Black cannot legally move his King.

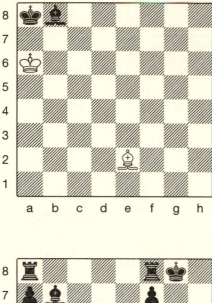

DIAGRAM 98

57. Black has just moved his Bishop next to his King and offered a draw. Should White accept?

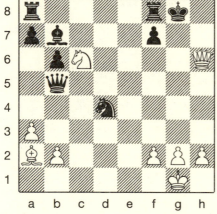

DIAGRAM 99

58. Should White try to draw by perpetual check?

57. White should not accept the draw offer because although material is perfectly even, he can checkmate by moving his Bishop one square to the right at f3. Black's last move was, of course, a terrible blunder in an otherwise totally drawn position.

58. If he wishes, White can draw by perpetual check. He need only shuffle his Queen from g6 to h6, back and forth in front of the Black King. Notice that the Black pawn by the King cannot capture the Queen when it checks on g6 because the pawn is pinned by White's Bishop in the left-hand corner of the board. Yet, White should not take a draw by perpetual because the check that his Knight has at e7 on the Black King is also checkmate.

3 *How to Write Down Chess Games*

O PEN ANY CHESS BOOK, and you see symbols that look like algebraic equations. They are not. These symbols are part of an exceedingly simple system of grid coordinates called *chess notation,* which permits players to write down their chess moves as they play them. In the next 60 seconds or so, you will understand all. Take a look at Diagram 100:

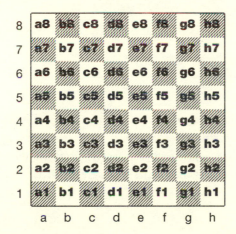

DIAGRAM 100

The notation system used in this book is called *algebraic,* and it is accepted in nearly all countries as a simple way of designating the squares of the chessboard and of representing the moves. The letters running from a to h below the board represent vertical columns that are called *files,* while the numbers to the left of the board denote horizontal rows that are called *ranks.* Simply run your finger up to, say, the number 4 and then move it to the right until it intersects with the e-file, and you land on the e4-square. Put an empty chessboard in front of you and practice for a minute or two by letting your eyes match up a rank and a file to pinpoint a given square. Then switch your eyes back to the above diagram to check your mental surmise. Continue switching back and forth from empty board to the diagram for another five minutes.

That's all there is to it.

In common chess talk, the squares from a1 to h1 are called the first rank, those from a2 to h2 are called the second rank, and so on. The squares from a1 to a8 are the a-file, those from b1 to b8 are the b-file, and so on. When the men are set up in their initial position as in Diagram 1 on page 12, the White pieces are on the first and second ranks, while the Black pieces are on the seventh and eighth ranks.

Another piece of chess talk is the word *diagonal.* In Diagram 101 there are four examples of diagonals.

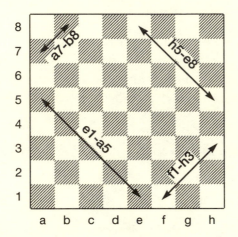

DIAGRAM 101

The squares comprising a given diagonal are obviously all of one color, and the phrases *light-square diagonal* and *dark-square diagonal* are common in chess literature as is the phrase *long diagonal,* which refers to the diagonal running all across the board from either a1 to h8 or from h1 to a8. All told, there are 26 diagonals ranging in length from two to eight squares.

WRITING DOWN MOVES

A *move* means transferring a piece from one square to another, and the convention in algebraic notation is to give the piece symbol and then the square of destination. Here is a table giving the symbols used in chess notation:

THIS SYMBOL	INDICATES
K	A King
Q	A Queen
R	A Rook
B	A Bishop
N	A Knight
x	A capture
+	Check
=	A pawn promotion to a designated piece
e.p.	*En passant* capture
0-0	Kingside castling
0-0-0	Queenside castling
...	White's move has been omitted
mate	Checkmate

We also use symbols to comment on the quality of the moves as well:

THIS SYMBOL	INDICATES
!	A good move
?	A bad move
!!	An excellent move
??	An awful move
!?	An interesting move
?!	An interesting but doubtful move

Here is how the system works in practice. If you start a game by moving the White pawn in front of the King two spaces, you write 1. e4 (a convention is that pawn moves do not require the letter "P"). If Black responds by moving the pawn in front of the Queen two spaces, you write 1. ... d5 (the three dots in front of d5 mean that Black made the move, and they are used only when writing Black's move without White's move in front of it). A capture by White on the next move is written 2. exd5.

In Chapter 1, you learned about promoting a pawn by advancing it to the other end of the board. The move 33. dxe8=Q+ indicates that, on his 33rd turn, White captured a piece on e8 with the d-pawn and promoted the pawn to a Queen while also checking the Black King. Another rule given in Chapter 1, capturing *en passant*, is represented in algebraic notation by the letters "*e.p.*" Thus, after 1. d4 c5 2. d5 e5, White can play 3. dxe6 *e.p.* Even though the Black pawn captured is on e5, you write "e6" because that square is the destination of White's capturing d-pawn. See Diagram 102.

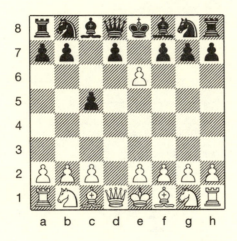

DIAGRAM 102

Here are the first seven moves of an opening called the Bogo-Indian Defense, leading to the position in Diagram 103:

1.	d4	Nf6
2.	c4	e6
3.	Nf3	Bb4+
4.	Nbd2	b6
5.	e3	Bb7
6.	a3	Bxd2+

7.   **Qxd2**   **0-0**

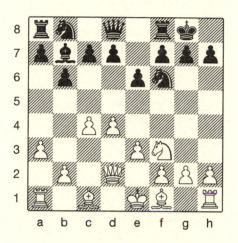

DIAGRAM 103

Notice that the notation for White's 4. Nbd2 contains the additional letter "b." Since White had the option of moving either his Knight on b1 or on f3 to d2 to block the check, it is necessary to indicate which Knight moved by the letter "b." If the other Knight had moved, then the notation would read 4. Nfd2. Black's 6. ... Bxd2+ means that the second player captured the White Knight on d2 and also delivered a check.

After doing the following exercises, turn to "Chess Movie: Practice Soon Makes Perfect" on page 76, play over the game, and write down the moves as given beneath each diagram.

DO YOUR EXERCISES

Knowing the chessboard well means winning more games. Mental exercises can firm up your grasp of the 64 squares. For example, starting with a White Knight on g1, try to imagine how it can get to f2 in two moves. The answer, of course, is Nh3 and then Nf2. Now, place a Knight on a1 and shift it around in your mind. Try to visualize the Knight going from a1 to h1 in five moves. One possible route is Nc2, Ne1, Nd3, Nf2, Nh1. Grab a pen and paper, and try these exercises:.

1. Turn to Diagram 1 on page 12 and write down the squares on which the White and Black men stand in the starting position. For example, write "White Rooks a1 and h1" and so on.

2. Place an empty chessboard as if you are White. What color are the following squares: b5, g5, c3, c6, e1, e8, d8, d1, b7, g2, h2, a7, a3, g8? Write "L" for light and "D" for dark.

3. Now place the board as if you are Black and give the colors of the following squares: d8, b7, g5, e1, g2, a7, c3, a3, b5, e8, c6, g8, d1, h2.

4. Which square along the long light diagonal intersects with the d-file? Which square along the c1-h6 diagonal is on the fifth rank?

The answers to these exercises are as follows:

1. For the White men: King, e1; Queen, d1; Rooks, a1 and h1; Bishops, c1 and f1; Knights, b1 and g1; pawns, a2 to h2. For the Black men: King, e8; Queen, d8; Rooks, a8 and h8; Bishops c8 and f8; Knights, b8 and g8; pawns a7 to h7.

2. L, D, D, L, D, L, D, L, L, L, D, D, D, L.

3. D, L, D, D, L, D, D, D, L, L, L, L, L, D. Did you notice that the squares in this exercise are the same as in the second exercise, only in a different order? If you misidentified any square, check to see if you answered correctly in exercise 2.

4. d5, g5.

In these exercises the objective is not to memorize the chessboard but to turn it into user-friendly territory. You will soon be able to visualize in your mind's eye the pieces in their initial positions, and without bothering to think about it, you will know that if White moves the King Knight on his first turn, then it must go to either f3 or h3.

Work out your own exercises. They are good for intellectual fitness.

CHESS MOVIE: PRACTICE SOON MAKES PERFECT

Set up the pieces in the starting position and grab a pen and some paper. You are about to record a chess game. Your partner is Mr. Dearman as Black in the game Davis–Dearman, played in the United States in 1902. Do not be annoyed by making elementary errors such as forgetting to write the "+" sign to indicate checks. Just play through the game below, write down the moves as given, and then you'll be ready to tackle the practice notation in Chapter 4. These exercises, coupled with recording a few of your own games, will quickly transform what appears to be an onerous task into an automatic routine. Where chess notation is concerned, practice—including this exercise in rote-work—soon makes almost perfect.

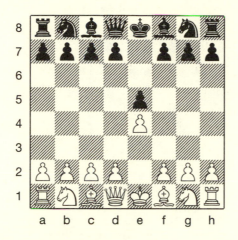

DIAGRAM 104

1. Write 1. e4 e5, and move the pawns as shown above (with White moving first).

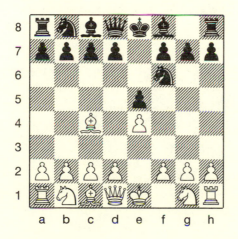

DIAGRAM 105

2. Now play 2. Bc4 Nf6, as shown above. Black is playing the Berlin Defense against White's Bishop Opening. The names of chess openings are colorful, but do not bother to memorize them at this point.

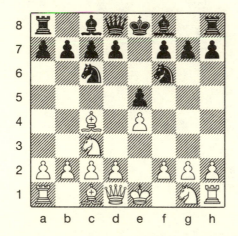

DIAGRAM 106

3. Write 3. Nc3 Nc6, and slide the White Knight to c3 and the Black Knight to c6. Notice how both sides pushed their pawns into the center of the board, while angling their pieces toward the center. They avoid moving the a- and h-pawns until later (or if at all).

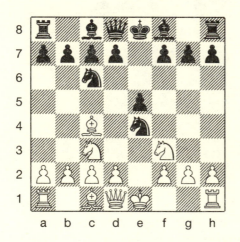

DIAGRAM 107

4. The next moves for White and Black are 4. Nf3 Nxe4. Write them down! Yes, Black captured White's pawn on e4 (the "x" indicates a capture). And yes, White can capture the Knight on e4, winning a Knight worth 3 points in return for a pawn worth only 1 point. But Mr. Dearman and you have a little surprise coming up.

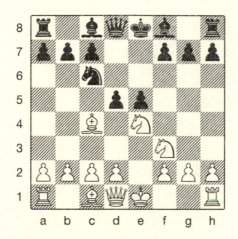

DIAGRAM 108

5. Here's the trick: After 5. Nxe4, Black retrieves the lost material by 5. ...
    d5, because the Black Queen pawn simultaneously attacks both the
    White Bishop on c4 and the White Knight on e4. Notice how all the
    action occurs in the vital center.

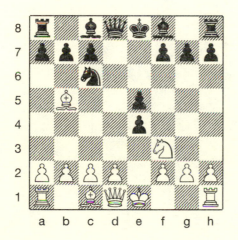

DIAGRAM 109

6. Faced with having to lose either his Knight or Bishop, White decides
    to save his Bishop by moving it to b5 (6. Bb5). Black hurriedly snaps
    off the horse on e4 (6. ... dxe4). For a moment, Black is up a pawn.
    Thus far, the Bishops and Knights, the so-called "minor" pieces, have
    been battling. Queens and then Rooks usually enter the game later.

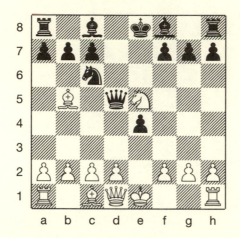

DIAGRAM 110

7. White has his own resource: He plays 7. Nxe5, restoring material equality. You cannot respond with 7. ... Nxe5 because White's Bishop on b5 could then capture your Black King on e8. Instead, Black centralizes his Queen with 7. ... Qd5, attacking White's two developed pieces.

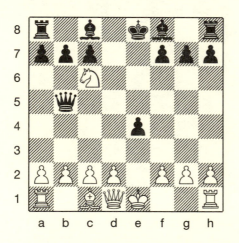

DIAGRAM 111

8. Write down the moves! This first exercise may seem difficult, but recording moves is nothing more than an easily mastered, low-grade form of symbol manipulation. Write down 8. Nxc6 Qxb5, and make the captures as shown above.

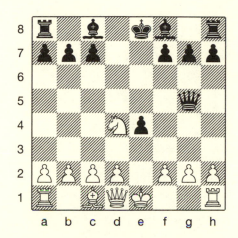

DIAGRAM 112

9.   Make the moves 9. Nd4 (getting the Knight out of danger and threat-
     ening to capture Black's Queen) 9. ... Qg5. Black now attacks White's
     unprotected pawn on g2. Material is even. Who stands better?

DIAGRAM 113

10. Black does. After 10. g3 Bg4, Black has two pieces developed, White
     only one. Further, the Black Queen is attacking rather than being
     attacked. White is in trouble.

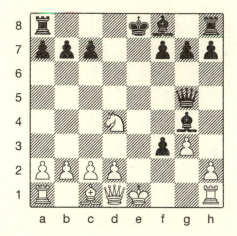

DIAGRAM 114

11. White plays 11. f3 to blunt the threat on his Queen from Black's Bishop on g4, and Black slays the foot soldier with 11. ... exf3. Your material advantage is temporary, but your edge in piece development is not. The Black Bishop on f8 is hot to trot, while White's is trapped on c1.

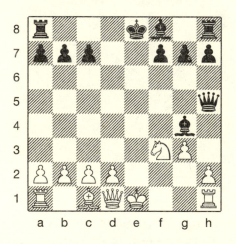

DIAGRAM 115

12. The moves are 12. Nxf3 Qh5. Material is level but not the position. Black threatens to rustle a piece with ... Bxf3, and the Knight on f3 is pinned because if it moves, Black wins decisive material by ... Bxd1. White must find a way to protect the horse.

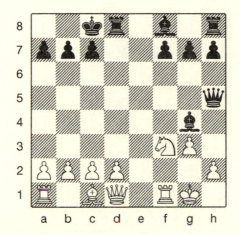

DIAGRAM 116

13. Hence 13. 0-0, the symbol for castling Kingside, which removes the White King from the center and adds the Rook to the defense of the Knight on f3. Black castles Queenside, 13. ... 0-0-0. Notice the light squares around White's King that are either vacant or attacked by Black's pieces.

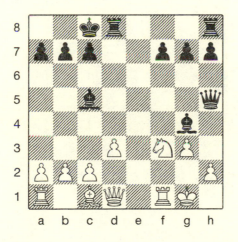

DIAGRAM 117

14. White tries 14. d3 to open up his Queen Bishop, and Black develops another piece with 14. ... Bc5+ (the plus sign indicates a check on White's King). Four of Black's five pieces are in action, while White's pieces are backward and tied down to defense. The knockout is four rounds of moves away.

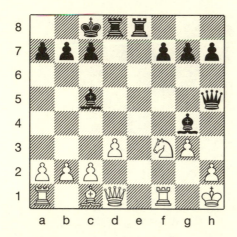

DIAGRAM 118

15. White must get out of check, and 15. Kh1 is the move. Black develops his last piece with 15. ... Rhe8. Black's Rooks rake the central d- and e-files, and both of his Bishops are active. Only White's Knight is beyond the second rank, and it is under attack.

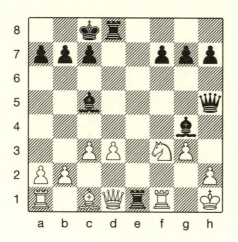

DIAGRAM 119

16. The first player tries 16. c3, intending to play 17. d4, blocking the Black Bishop on c5, which is currently sweeping down the a7-g1 diagonal, directly into White's porous Kingside. But Black brushes aside this feeble defensive parry with 16. ... Re1!!, a stunning punch.

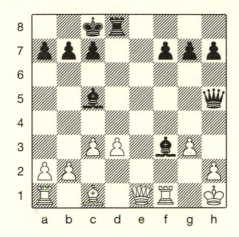

DIAGRAM 120

17. In a daze, White knows he must capture the Black intruder on e1, but how to do so? On 17. Rxe1, Black puts away the opponent with 17. ... Bxf3+ 18. Qxf3 (forced to relieve check) 18. ... Qxf3 mate. Instead White tries 17. Qxe1, but Black hits hard with 17. ... Bxf3+.

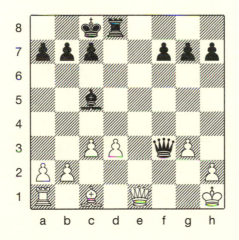

DIAGRAM 121

18. White is forced to play 18. Rxf3, since his King cannot go to g1 because the Bishop at c5 is bearing down on that square. You and your partner finish the game with 18. ... Qxf3 mate. White's King cannot escape capture.

Check your transcription of algebraic notation in the preceding chess movie against this correct score of A. Davis–Dearman:

A. DAVIS–DEARMAN

1.	e4	e5
2.	Bc4	Nf6
3.	Nc3	Nc6
4.	Nf3	Nxe4
5.	Nxe4	d5
6.	Bb5	dxe4
7.	Nxe5	Qd5
8.	Nxc6	Qxb5
9.	Nd4	Qg5
10.	g3	Bg4
11.	f3	exf3
12.	Nxf3	Qh5
13.	0-0	0-0-0
14.	d3	Bc5+
15.	Kh1	Rhe8
16.	c3	Re1
17.	Qxe1	Bxf3+
18.	Rxf3	Qxf3 mate

4 *Chess Movie: The "Write" Moves*

PEN AND PAPER READY, board at hand with pieces set up in the beginning position? It's time to show you've got the "write stuff" when it comes to recording chess games. Your job is to record the moves in the order described beneath each diagram. But this time we won't be showing you the notation as we describe the moves — you must write down the notation for yourself.

CAPA-TIVATINGLY SIMPLE PLAY

As White, your partner will be Jose Raul Capablanca (1888–1942), the
Cuban chess prodigy who was world champion from 1921 to 1927. In this
"lost" masterpiece, which here appears for the first time in book form, you
will marvel at how the immortal "Capa" invades with his Rooks along the
d-file, wins a pawn, and makes victory look easy. The great Cuban was
often called "the Mozart of chess," and he was justifiably famous for his
masterful yet capa-tivatingly simple play. Your opponent: Juan Corzo. The
backdrop: Havana, July 23, 1909.

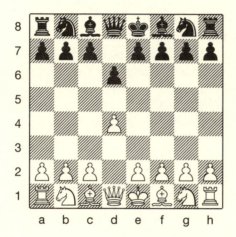

DIAGRAM 122

1. Take a look at the above diagram. White moves the pawn in front of
   his Queen two squares, and Black responds by moving the pawn in
   front of his Queen one square. Write 'em down. The opening of this
   game is rare and has no name. Chess writers usually call such a debut
   an "Irregular Opening."

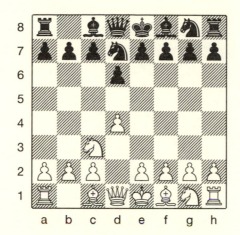

DIAGRAM 123

2. Did you write down the pawn moves in Diagram 122? Now do the same for the Knight moves in this diagram. As in the two earlier chess movies, both players strive to develop their minor pieces—Bishops and Knights—first. Queens and then Rooks usually, though not always, come later.

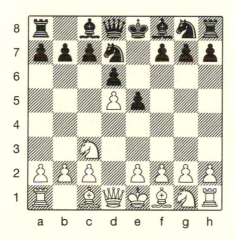

DIAGRAM 124

3. White advances his Queen pawn one square, and Black stakes out space in the center by playing his King pawn forward two squares. Do you recall the *en passant* rule? You are about to see an example in Diagram 125. Notice how both sides put their pieces and pawns in the center.

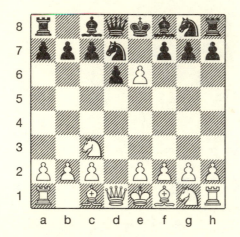

DIAGRAM 125

4. White captures Black's King pawn *en passant*. Here is a hint for recording the move: Take a gander at what square White's former d-pawn now occupies. Unlike the earlier two games, there are no fireworks in this one. Capablanca was famous for quiet though deadly play.

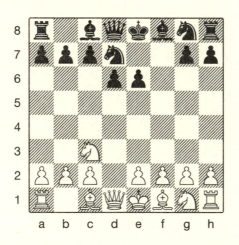

DIAGRAM 126

5. Black snaps off the White intruder on e6. Write it down. Do not forget that for a great master such as Capablanca the winning of a single pawn or the creation of a single weakness in the opponent's position is enough for victory. This famous Cuban player was called "the chess machine." No one ever played more accurately.

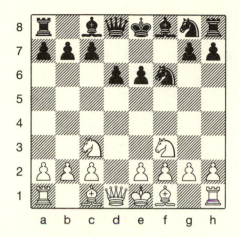

DIAGRAM 127

6. White moves his King Knight, and Black responds by moving his Queen Knight as shown.

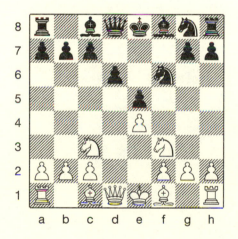

DIAGRAM 128

7. Now both White and Black advance their King pawns as shown. "Capa," as he was known affectionately, has more scope for his Queen than Black has for his lady.

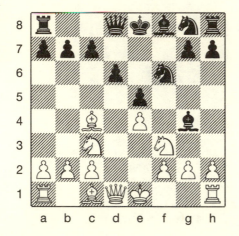

DIAGRAM 129

8. White sorties his King Bishop and Black his Queen Bishop. Check the diagram and record your moves. Notice how your White Bishop strikes the light squares at e6 and f7. Black's King is stuck in the center with little hope of castling. Top players often win by accumulating such small advantages.

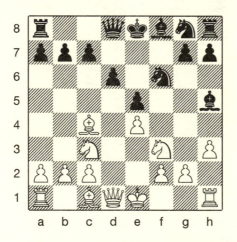

DIAGRAM 130

9. White nudges Black's Bishop by playing his King Rook pawn up one square, and Black retreats the Bishop.

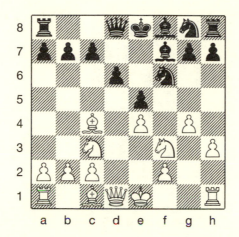

DIAGRAM 131

10. White harasses the Black Bishop again by advancing his g-pawn two squares, and Black further retreats his Bishop as shown. While Black's Kingside pieces are constricted and bunched together, White's open position provides lots of room for his pieces.

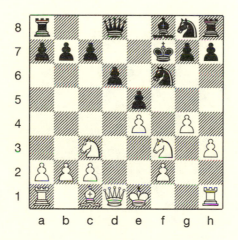

DIAGRAM 132

11. White takes the Black Bishop with check, and Black recaptures with his King, which having moved can no longer castle. As in the Davis–Dearman game on page 86, both players develop their Bishops and Knights first, while the Rooks come into play later. As a general rule, that is sound strategy.

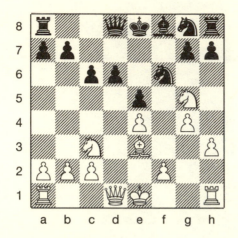

DIAGRAM 133

12. Each side makes two moves in the above diagram. First, White checks with his Knight, and Black moves his King back to its original square. White then develops his Queen Bishop to e3, and Black tries to contest the center by moving his c-pawn up one square. White now has three pieces developed, Black only one.

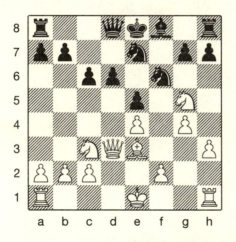

DIAGRAM 134

13. White advances his Queen to prepare for Queenside castling, and Black tries to develop his King Knight from g8. White's Knight on g5 attacks the e6 and f7 squares near Black's King. Black has only one piece beyond his second rank compared to four for White.

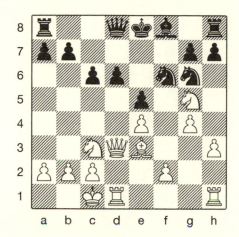

DIAGRAM 135

14. White castles Queenside, thereby ushering his King to a safe haven, bringing his Rook onto the central d-file, and connecting both Rooks. He now attacks the d-pawn with two pieces. Black unblocks his Bishop by moving the Knight from e7. Count 'em: White has five pieces developed, Black two.

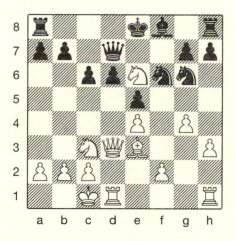

DIAGRAM 136

15. Capa sees a short sequence of moves—a *combination*—that will win the d-pawn. He sinks his Knight into e6, attacking the Black Queen, which moves as shown. White's pieces have loads of room in which to maneuver, while Black's pieces are constricted.

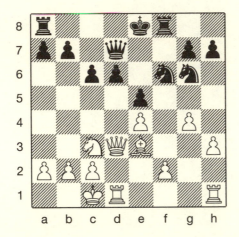

DIAGRAM 137

16. White trades his strong Knight on e6 for the hemmed in Black cleric on f8, a bad idea at first glance. But after Black takes the Knight with his Rook, White still has two pieces attacking the d-pawn, and Black has only one defending because of the elimination of his Bishop. Capa cashes in by winning material.

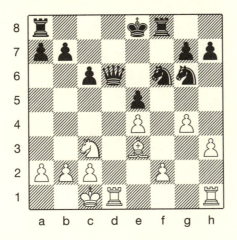

DIAGRAM 138

17. White pockets the d-pawn with his Queen, and Black responds by taking the White Queen with his own lady. For just a moment, Black is up a Queen, but White is on move and will soon rectify the imbalance. Virtually all of the action has been in the center of the board.

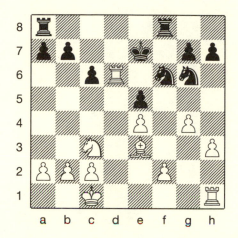

DIAGRAM 139

18. Capa captures Black's Queen, and Black moves up his King to challenge the White Rook and to connect his own castles. Black wants to challenge White's control of the open d-file, while White's idea is to exchange pieces and advance his extra pawn to the eighth rank for a new Queen.

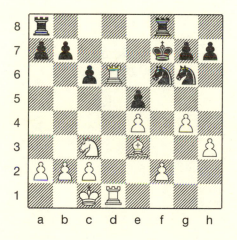

DIAGRAM 140

19. Because his Rooks are connected, White can slide over his King Rook to guard his Rook on d6, thereby "doubling" on the central d-file. Black glides his King laterally to escape possible attacks. Take a gander: White is up a pawn, and his pieces control the center.

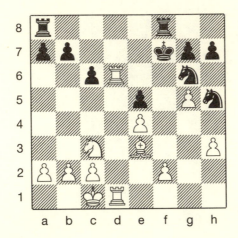

DIAGRAM 141

20. A new combination is brewing to win a second pawn. Capa thrusts forward his g-pawn, attacking the Black steed at f6 and forcing it to the side of the board. White is centralizing, Black is decentralizing. In addition, Black no longer has a Knight guarding the d7-square. Watch.

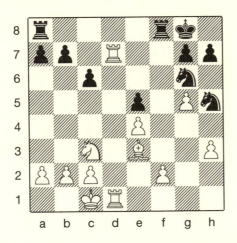

DIAGRAM 142

21. White's Rook plays a check on d7, and Black removes his monarch to g8, thereby artificially castling, which is a phrase denoting that he took several moves to accomplish what could be done in a single play. White will now pick off Black's exceedingly ripe Queenside pawns.

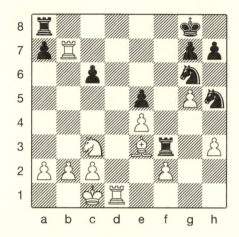

DIAGRAM 143

22. White's Rook captures the b-pawn, and Black tries a counterattack on the Kingside by advancing his Rook on the f-file. But it is too late. White has two extra pawns and will soon scurry forward with his a-pawn, intending to make a new Queen on a8.

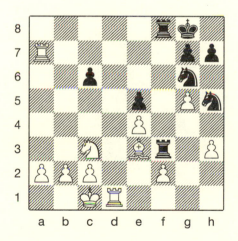

DIAGRAM 144

23. The first player devours the a-pawn with his Rook, which is guarded by the Bishop on e3. Black withdraws his Queen Rook and doubles along the f-file, just as White did along the d-file in Diagram 140. White has just finished mopping up on the Queenside, while Black's Rooks are still in the bucket.

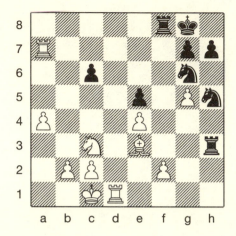

DIAGRAM 145

24. Capa thrusts forward his a-pawn, and Black's Rook goes fishing for the h-pawn. White is still up two pawns and is preparing to promote the a-pawn. Still worse for Black, he has no reasonable plan to disrupt this ceremony, since his pieces are all on the opposite side of the board.

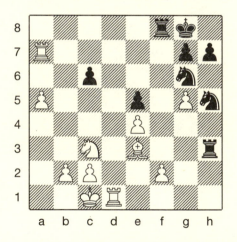

DIAGRAM 146

25. Pretend you are the immortal Cuban and move the a-pawn forward one square. You are now only three squares away from making a Queen. Capa's opponent, who was once Cuban champion, understands that he cannot stop the a-pawn and knows that his opponent will not commit a crude blunder.

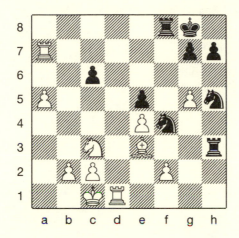

DIAGRAM 147

26. Hence his decision to play his g-Knight to f4 and then to resign the game without waiting for a reply.

Have you recorded every move as described? Did you remember to use x's for captures and the plus sign for checks? Compare your score with this correct version:

JOSE CAPABLANCA–JUAN CORZO

1.	d4	d6
2.	Nc3	Nd7
3.	d5	e5
4.	dxe6 *e.p.*	fxe6
5.	Nf3	Ndf6
6.	e4	e5
7.	Bc4	Bg4
8.	h3	Bh5
9.	g4	Bf7
10.	Bxf7+	Kxf7
11.	Ng5+	Ke8
12.	Be3	c6
13.	Qd3	Ne7

14.	0-0-0	Ng6
15.	Ne6	Qd7
16.	Nxf8	Rxf8
17.	Qxd6	Qxd6
18.	Rxd6	Ke7
19.	Rhd1	Kf7
20.	g5	Nh5
21.	Rd7+	Kg8
22.	Rxb7	Rf3
23.	Rxa7	Raf8
24.	a4	Rxh3
25.	a5	Ngf4, and Black resigns

How to Open a Chess Game

THE OPENING OF A CHESS GAME comprises about the first 10 or 15 moves by each side. More books have been written on the opening—indeed, many thousands—than on any other part of chess.

Most of these books are worthless to any player below the master level; they are written with the not ignoble motive of enriching authors and, as is the case of much academic writing in many fields, to establish a given author's reputation among his peers. These books are not written to improve the play of the average chess enthusiast. Indeed, the average chessplayer spends years mindlessly memorizing hundreds of specific sequences of moves given in these thick compendiums of opening knowledge and then wonders why after all of this labor and after all of the promises contained in the advertising, he plays only a bit better.

Before studying specific opening variations, which in a few instances may stretch out to 30 moves, a student should learn the key principles of opening play. For every game that a student loses to a "booked-up" opponent who springs a carefully concealed trap given in some opening book, he wins 10 against the same opponent by understanding basic principles and applying them.

THE BEST OPENING PLAN

There is no "best" opening or "best" defense to cover every contingency; there are instead dozens of major openings that involve thousands of attacks and defenses. Yet there is a best opening plan: Play to occupy and control the center and, eventually, the so-called extended center.

In Diagram 148, the area within the smaller square is, quite simply, the *center*—the d4, d5, e4 and e5 squares. The area within the larger square is the *extended center.*

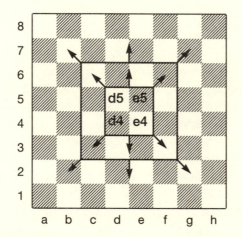

DIAGRAM 148

Notice the arrows in the diagram. They suggest the reason why the center (in this book, we use this phrase also to encompass the squares of the extended center) is so important: From a central point, it is possible to radiate influence outward. By controlling the center, you enjoy three major advantages:

1. *Mobility.* Pieces in the center are more mobile than their brothers on the edges because they can move to more squares. For example, consider the Knight. On its starting block of g1, the White King Knight can move to three squares (e2, f3, h3). When moved to f3 (toward the center), the King Knight can suddenly control eight squares. On the

other hand, moving the Knight to h3, away from the center, leaves the piece controlling only four squares. Now put the Knight on any of the four corner squares (a1, a8, h1 or h8): It controls only two squares.

A more subtle example of how central control confers mobility is given in Diagram 149. This position is reached after 1. e4 h5 2. d4 a5.

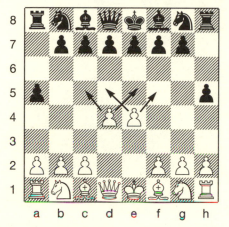

DIAGRAM 149

Here is the score after only two moves: Each of White's central pawns controls two squares (the d-pawn controls c5 and e5, and the e-pawn controls d5 and f5), while Black's flank pawns control one square each. But the situation is still more lopsided. By moving his two center pawns, White has opened up his Queen, which suddenly surveys six squares, and his two Bishops, which can move to a total of 10 squares. Add up the total: White is hitting 20 squares. As for Black, his two Rooks command four squares, which when added to the two earlier pawn-controlled squares, give Black six all told.

Square-counting is mechanical thinking, and it can be crude. At times, the quantity of squares controlled is less important than the quality. Still, the scoreboard reads 20–6 after only two moves. Moreover, there is nothing wrong with the quality of White's squares, most of which butchers would label as prime center cuts.

2. *Restriction.* Pawns and pieces in the center restrict the ability of the opponent to organize his forces because they act as a barrier to the development of the other side.

3. *Combat Readiness.* The geometry of the 64 squares permits pieces in the center to move more quickly to either side of the chessboard. To continue with the opening moves in Diagram 149: 3. Nf3 Nh6 4. Nc3 Na6. The resulting position:

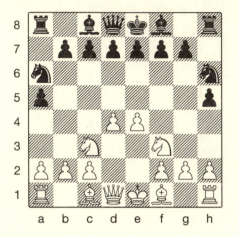

DIAGRAM 150

In addition to White increasing his lead in mobility, he also possesses tremendous flexibility. Depending on future fortunes, his Knights may quickly head toward any part of the board. Thus, White's Queen Knight can reach the Kingside in a single move, while in the best of circumstances, Black's Queen Knight will require two moves. Black's Knights have the single option of moving toward the center, each accomplishing in two or three moves what White accomplished in one move for each Knight.

The capacity to zing pieces from one sector of the board to another is often decisive. Indeed, if the above position existed between two amateurs of medium strength, the player handling Black would have to play top-notch chess for the remainder of the game to avoid defeat.

BUILDING THE CENTER

A good position for White in the center often looks similar to a good position for Black. In this chapter, for the sake of simplicity, many of the examples feature the White pieces. But Black can also get the good things in chess life, though he must work a bit harder because he moves second.

Here is an ideal opening development for either Black or White:

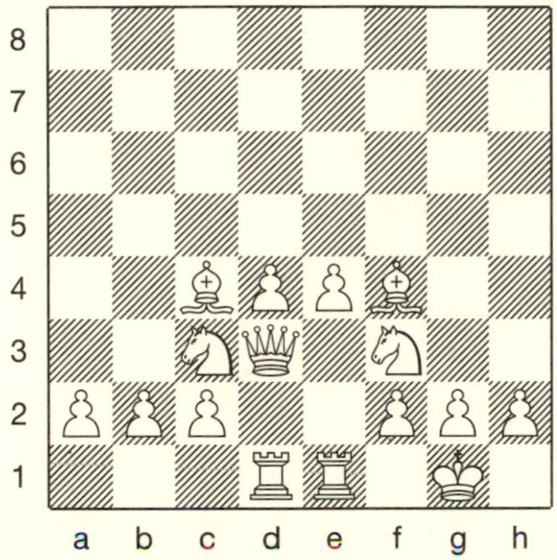

DIAGRAM 151

The preferred order of moves to reach the above position suggests several general rules for opening deployment.

First, the moves: 1. e4, 2. d4, 3. Nf3, 4. Bc4, 5. Nc3, 6. Bf4, 7. 0-0, 8. Qd3, 9. Re1, 10. Rd1.

Second, the general rules governing this move order:

1. Move the center pawns to stake out territory. The e-pawn goes first so you can develop your Kingside pieces with maximum speed and then castle.

2. Knights should usually be developed before Bishops, which explains 3. Nf3. The move 4. Bc4 comes before 5. Nc3 because it's best to prepare for castling as soon as possible. In general, place White Knights on c3 and f3 and Black Knights on c6 and f6.

3. As soon as the minor pieces (the Knights and Bishops) are developed, castle. Castling activates a Rook and tucks your King away on one side of the board, where it is generally safer than in the middle.

4. Only after developing the minor pieces and castling do you move the Queen, which connects the Rooks.

5. The Rooks are the last pieces to enter the fray. Rooks usually do their best work when developed quickly on the central files at e1 and d1 (or e8 and d8 for Black) rather than along the vertical edges of the a- and h-files.

The above method of building and controlling the center involves occupying the central squares directly with pawns and pieces. It is called *classical chess*. Another method of controlling the center is called *hypermodern chess*, which became popular shortly after World War I. Here is a typical hypermodern style of development:

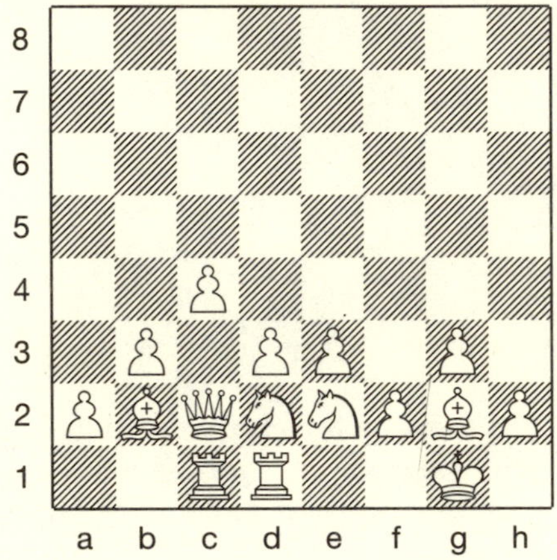

DIAGRAM 152

Hypermodernism is characterized above all by attempting to control the center by the influence of pieces—usually Bishops—developed on the flanks. Notice how the Bishops at b2 and g2 are aimed toward the center and can actually crisscross all four squares of the core center. Control, but do not occupy (at least right away) is the hypermodern motto. A move in the opening that develops a Bishop on b2 or g2 or on b7 or g7 is called a *fianchetto*.

The above examples of center building represent the ideal. For example, in the diagram of the classical center (Diagram 151), White moved every piece only once, and both of his pawn moves opened lines for his pieces. When facing the moves of a breathing opponent, White will not have so easy a time. He may have to move the same piece twice or even three times to reach the optimum central square, and he may also be forced to move his a- or h-pawn at some point, which adds little to his development.

SPEEDY AND HEALTHY DEVELOPMENT

In chess language, *development* means moving pieces to better squares or moving pawns to open lines for pieces. In the opening, development means moving pawns and pieces off the first and second ranks for White (or seventh and eighth for Black) so that they can become fighting units in the center and, later on, in the opponent's territory.

Beyond directing one's pieces toward the center, the cardinal rule of opening development is to try to move each piece once before moving any piece twice. Exceptions to this rule include capturing an opponent's man advantageously, recapturing a man in a trade, and creating a dangerous threat that is difficult to defend. The more pieces that are moved only once, the more quickly one completes development.

The reason for developing rapidly is that the player who first succeeds in bringing his pieces into play can obviously start attacking before his opponent can, giving him better chances of winning the game.

By combining the ideas of centralization and development when making opening moves, one can formulate a comprehensive principle guiding opening play: Develop pawns and pieces toward the center.

Speed in development is fine, but speed without regard to healthy good sense can kill. You have already learned not to develop the Queen before the minor pieces, yet many players are tempted to do so with the thought that speedy development of the most powerful piece must make sense in spite of warnings posted by virtually all chess teachers.

A second corrupting thought is the lure of gaining a quick victory by attacking an opponent with the Queen, hoping that he will not be able to defend against the threats. One short game that every beginning player has both won and lost starts with:

1.	e4	e5
2.	Qh5?	g6??

A good defense here is 2. ... Nc6 3. Bc4 g6 (see the game starting on page 110), followed by the fianchetto, 4. ... Bg7, when Black suddenly has more pieces developed than White!

3.	Qxe5+	Qe7
4.	Qxh8	

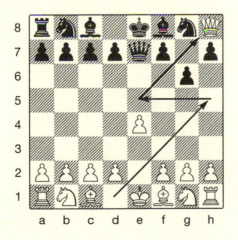

DIAGRAM 153

White is up a Rook and should win the game fairly easily. Notice the zig-zag course followed by the White Queen.

The Queen sortie seen most often in opening play occurs in what is known as Scholar's Mate:

1.	e4	e5
2.	Bc4	Nc6
3.	Qh5	Nf6??
4.	Qxf7 mate	

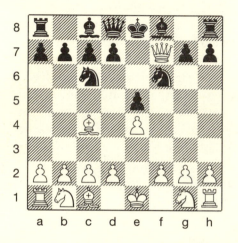

DIAGRAM 154

Once again White has triumphed easily by developing his Queen first and checkmating Black shortly thereafter. Yet he is violating a fundamental principle by moving his Queen so early and can be punished relatively easily.

Here is how Black could have refuted White's play:

1.	e4	e5
2.	Bc4	Nc6
3.	Qh5	g6

Black defends against 4 Qxf7 mate.

4.	Qf3	Nf6

With his fourth move, White again threatens Qxf7 mate, and Black again defends.

5.	g4	Nd4

White wants to play 6. g5, hitting Black's Knight, and when it moves, to play 7. Qxf7 mate. Instead, Black counterattacks with a double threat: to capture the White Queen and to win White's Rook with 6. ... Nxc2+ and 7. ... Nxa1.

6.	Qd1	

On 6. Qd3, Black can win a pawn by 6. ... Nxg4 or, still better, can continue attacking with 6. ... d5, as in the game. The Queen retreat back to d1 is the only way to keep material even.

| 6. | ... | d5 |

Everything is going wrong for White. He has moved the same piece three times in the opening, and it is back on its original square. Notice how Black has furthered his development by using his Knight to attack the Queen, thereby forcing it to move. Black also has open lines for both of his Bishops, while White has only one Bishop able to move.

| 7. | exd5 | Bxg4 |

Black's lead in development and more open lines for his pieces are now quite striking. And once again, Black develops a minor piece, the Bishop, while simultaneously attacking the White Queen. The precise count: Black has three pieces developed, White only one.

DIAGRAM 155

| 8. | f3 |

White must prevent the loss of his Queen. On 8. Ne2, Black plays 8. ... Nf3+ 9. Kf1 Bh3 mate. And if 8. Be2, Black has 8. ... Qxd5, winning a pawn and threatening to take White's Rook on h1.

| 8. | ... | Ne4! |

A beautiful move that unleashes his Queen against White's King.

| 9. | fxg4 | Qh4+ |
| 10. | Kf1 | Qf2 mate |

By driving White's Queen around the board and developing his own pieces while doing so, Black transformed a four-move loss in the previous game into a win by checkmate in only 10 moves. The process of driving the Queen around the board allowed Black to win about four *tempos*, which is a chess term for the value of a chess move or the turn consumed in making that move.

If you wonder why it was good for Black to move some of his pieces twice in the opening (such as 5. ... Nd4), he did so to improve the position of the Knight and to attack the Black Queen, a maneuver that enabled him to further his development.

Remember: The general rule not to move the same piece twice in the opening is a general rule. Plenty of exceptions exist. If the opponent puts a piece where it may be captured for free, then of course move the same piece twice or thrice to win decisive material. And if, as in this game, you can further your development and create an attack by moving the same piece twice, then by all means do so.

BE A ROYALIST

Centralization and development are worthless as opening principles unless they are complemented by an abiding solicitude for King safety. When playing the opening, be a royalist.

An opening principle among chess wags is to castle early and castle often. Of course, you can castle only once during a game, but the hyperbole makes the point. You may play a textbook opening perfectly, but if you overlook a threat against your King by an opponent otherwise in desperate straits, you lose.

Castling should occur as soon as possible after moving one or two center pawns and developing two or three minor pieces. Try to castle within the first 10 moves, which usually means developing the Kingside Knight and Bishop before the Queenside pieces. If the opening develops so that you delay Kingside castling, you may have an opportunity for Queenside castling. When in doubt as to the better move, castle on the Kingside, where the King will be safer. On g1 or g8, the King guards the h-pawn, whereas in Queenside castling the King lands on c1 or c8, leaving the a-pawn underprotected.

THE EVILS OF PAWN-GRUBBING

In opening play, one of the most pernicious evils is mindlessly grabbing enemy pawns while the opponent develops his pieces. Chess people refer to this materialism as pawn-grubbing, and a common scenario is that one side will roam around the board eating pawns with his Queen. By move 10 or so, the opponent has four or five pieces developed, and the pawn-eater has only his Queen in play.

A rule of thumb: Three tempos are worth a pawn. In the following game, White is down three pawns by move 10, but a professional would calculate that the value of White's development when measured by tempos gives him a huge surplus.

1.	e4	e5
2.	d4	exd4
3.	c3	dxc3
4.	Bc4	cxb2
5.	Bxb2	

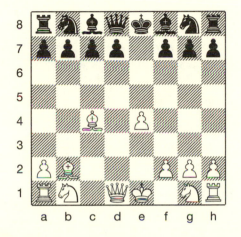

DIAGRAM 156

A dramatic contrast. Black has won a pair of pawns, but White has two raking Bishops bearing down on the center and Black's Kingside. And, of course, Black has not developed a single piece, though he does have open lines for his Queen and Bishop. The position is roughly even, with White having the value of nearly six moves in this position, keeping in mind not only the well-developed Bishops but also the free and open Queen and a King nearer to castling than Black's monarch.

The opening is called the Danish Gambit. A *gambit* is a voluntary surrender or sacrifice of material—usually a pawn—in the opening, which is designed to take the initiative or start an attack.

	5.	...	Bb4+

Dangerous for Black. White's Bishop on b2 now attacks Black's undefended g-pawn and, possibly, the Rook on h8. A solid defense begins with 5. ... d5, intending to give back one or perhaps both of the pawns to achieve full piece development (for the same idea, see move 8 of the Denker–Shayne chess movie at the end of this chapter). A possible line is 6. Bxd5 Bb4+ 7. Nc3 Bxc3+ 8. Bxc3 Nf6 9. Nf3 Nxd5 10. exd5 Qe7+ with an equal game.

6.	Nd2	Qg5?

Black violates the injunction against early development of the Queen, but he hopes to win White's pawn on g2 or, if White obliges, to trade Queens by 7. ... Qxd2+. Black would then be up two pawns, and White would not have enough remaining attacking force to compensate him for the two pawns.

7.	Nf3	Qxg2

Pawn-grubbing of the most greedy kind.

8.	Rg1	Bxd2+
9.	Ke2!	

An unpleasant surprise for Black, who had probably expected 9. Qxd2 Qxf3 or 9. Nxd2 Qxg1+ or 9. Kxd2 Qxf2+. Black must now move his Queen.

9.	...	Qh3
10.	Qxd2	

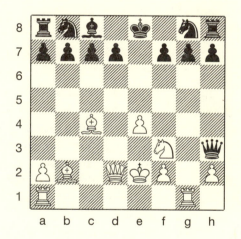

DIAGRAM 157

Black has three extra pawns and a Queen perched on the cliff at h3. Otherwise, none of his remaining pieces have moved! White, on the other hand, has every piece well-developed except for the Queen Rook. The game is over shortly.

10.	...	Nf6
11.	Bxf7+	Kd8

If 11. ... Kxf7, White wins the Queen by 12. Ng5+. On 11. ... Kf8, White also wins the Queen after 12. Ba3+ d6 13. Bxd6+ cxd6 14. Qxd6+ Kxf7 15. Ng5+.

12.	Rxg7	Nxe4

DIAGRAM 158

13.	Qg5+!	Nxg5
14.	Bf6 mate	

A preachment on foraging.

GETTING STARTED THE RIGHT WAY

Centralization, rapid development and King safety are the Big Three of opening principles. In practice you should begin games with the moves 1. e4 e5 or 1. d4 d5. Do not start out with 1. g4 g5, 1. h4 h5 and so on. If an opponent plays 1. g4 or 1. h4 then reply with 1. ... e5 or 1. ... d5. Think center.

Here is an example of correct opening play by both White and Black:

1.	e4	e5
2.	Nf3	Nc6
3.	Bc4	Nf6
4.	Nc3	Bb4
5.	0-0	0-0

6.   d3   d6

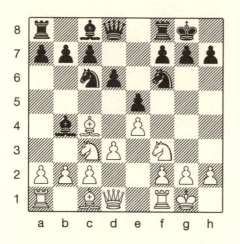

DIAGRAM 159

Both sides have acceptable positions, and the outcome of the game depends on who plays better later on.

THE DO'S OF OPENING PLAY

1. Begin the game by moving the e-pawn or, for variety, the d-pawn.

2. Try to establish a strong pawn center by occupying d4 and e4 with pawns.

3. Develop the minor pieces first (usually Knights before Bishops). And shortly after castling, develop the Queen and then the Rooks.

4. Castle early, preferably directly after developing the Kingside Knight and Bishop.

5. In general, develop the Kingside pieces before the Queenside pieces.

6. Develop pieces toward the center.

7. Unless there is a reason otherwise, move each piece once before moving any piece twice.

8. Try to make the first move of your Queen Rook to d1 or d8 and the first move of your King Rook to e1 or e8. Or, move your Rooks to any available open file.

9. The initial moves of the White and Black Knights should usually be to c3 or c6 and f3 or f6.

10. When moving a man, check to see if the opponent can capture it. If he can, check to see that the man is guarded and that you can recapture. Finally, check to see if the trade of pieces is in your favor (winning, say, a Rook for a Bishop) or at least relatively neutral (say, a Knight for a Bishop).

THE DONT'S OF OPENING PLAY

1. Unless there is a strong reason to the contrary, do not move one piece repeatedly at the expense of leaving other pieces undeveloped.

2. Do not play passive pawn moves remote from the center such as a2-a3 or ... a7-a6 and h2-h3 or ... h7-h6. These moves do not contest the center and do not open lines for the Bishops and Queens.

3. Do not delay castling.

4. Do not move the Queen before developing the minor pieces.

5. Do not play the White Knights to a3 and h3 or the Black Knights to a6 and h6.

6. Do not attack prematurely. Develop center pawns and pieces, castle and then advance to the attack.

7. Do not move one piece around the board, trying to grab the opponent's pawns, while he develops all of his pieces.

8. Do not move the f-pawn, especially before castling, unless there is a compelling reason. This move often permits attacks against the King (such as 1. f3? e5 2. g4?? Qh4 mate).

9. Do not try to develop White Rooks at a3 and h3 or Black Rooks at a6 and h6. They belong on d1 and e1 for White or d8 and e8 for Black.

10. Do not move a piece before checking to see if it can be taken.

CHESS MOVIE: FIRSTEST WITH THE MOSTEST

Napoleon won many battles by getting there firstest with the mostest, which is also how chess masters often win games. Your co-general as White is Grandmaster (or GM) Arnold Denker, U.S. Chess Champion from 1944 to 1946 and today known as the Grand Old Man of American Chess. White marches his men right into the center and mates the Black monarch right out of the opening. On move 11, Black disregards chessic folk wisdom, "When in doubt, castle," and keeps his King in the center, where it suffers the accustomed mating mortification. Your opponent as

Black is a Mr. Shayne, one of about 20 opponents whom GM Denker was playing simultaneously. The scene: Rochester, New York, 1945. The initial moves in this Bishop's Opening are 1. e4 e5 2. Bc4 Bc5 to reach the position given in Diagram 160.

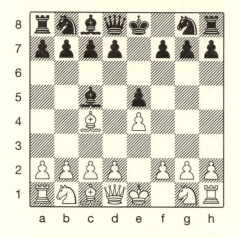

DIAGRAM 160

1. Winning material from the opponent is important in chess. But infinitely more important is ultimate victory by winning the opponent's King. That is the idea behind White's 3. b4, offering a pawn in return for quick development. Black grabs the foot soldier by 3. ... Bxb4.

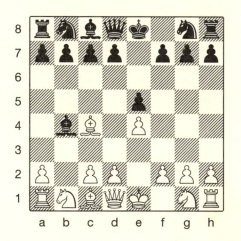

DIAGRAM 161

2. GM Denker attacks in the center with 4. c3 and threatens to capture Black's Bishop, which must move. Black plays 4. ... Bc5.

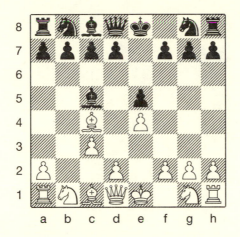

DIAGRAM 162

3. After 5. d4 exd4, Black has two extra pawns, but White has open lines not only for his Bishop on c4 but most notably for his Queen and dark-squared Bishop.

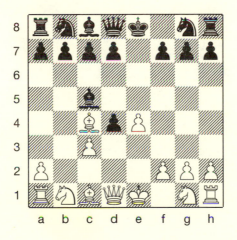

DIAGRAM 163

4. The name of the game is developing the pieces quickly, and there follows 6. Nf3 Nf6.

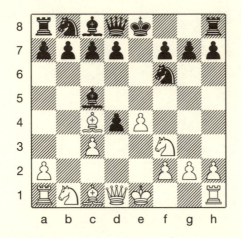

DIAGRAM 164

5. White keeps up relentless pressure with 7. e5, but Black puts up a fight with 7. ... Ne4. Will the open lines for White's Queen and Queen Bishop, not to mention the power of his Bishop on c4 striking Black at f7, compensate for the material deficit?

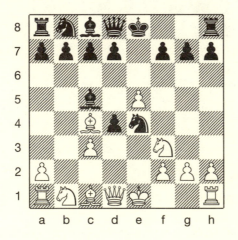

DIAGRAM 165

6. White protects his King and activates his Rook with 8. 0-0, and Black errs with 8. ... Nxc3. With the typical pawn sacrifice, 8. ... d5! 9. exd6 *e.p.* 0-0, Black could get his King to safety. Instead, he thrice moves his King Knight only to trade it for the unmoved White Knight.

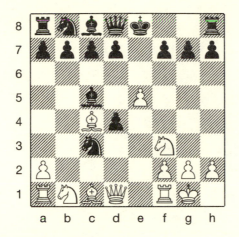

DIAGRAM 166

7. An interlude. White plays 9. Nxc3, and Black recaptures with 9. ... dxc3. White has castled, has developed his Knight and King Bishop, and enjoys open lines for his Queen and Queen Bishop. Black has a Bishop on c5 out. The verdict: White's development far outweighs his material minus.

DIAGRAM 167

8. There is a speedy win with 10. Qd5! Qe7 (White threatens both 11. Qxf7 mate and 11. Qxc5) 11. Bg5 Qf8, but GM Denker, who was playing 20 other games at the same time, tried 10. Bg5 Be7 11. Qd5, threatening 12. Qxf7, mate. The difference between this position and the suggested line is that Black can now ...

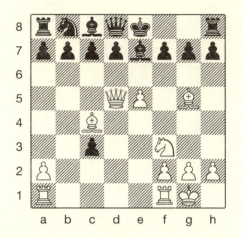

DIAGRAM 168

9. ... castle with 11. ... 0-0, removing his King from the center with good defensive chances. Instead, Black blunders with 11. ... Rf8??, and White plays 12. Bf6, which is like cramming a stick of dynamite into Black's innards. The threat is 13. Bxg7 Rg8 14. Qxf7 mate. Black is lost.

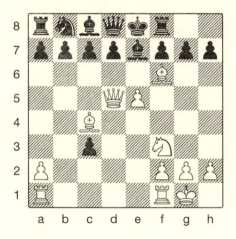

DIAGRAM 169

10. Temptation has killed many a chessplayer. Black plays 12. ... gxf6, lured by material riches. He could have offered more resistance by 12. ... Bxf6 13. exf6 Qxf6 14. Rfe1+ Kd8. U.S. Champion Denker knows fatal greed when he sees it and responds with 13. exf6.

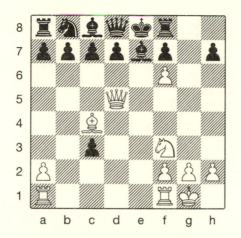

DIAGRAM 170

11. Black has only the hope that White will misplay the final attack. He tries 13. ... Bxf6, and White gets his King Rook into action along the central e-file with 14. Rfe1+ Be7 15. Ng5. The threat is 16. Nxf7 Rxf7 17. Qxf7 mate. White's lead in development is optically striking and decisive.

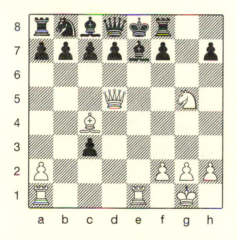

DIAGRAM 171

12. Knowing that the threat of 16. Nxf7 cannot be prevented, Black tries to drive off White's Queen with 15. ... c6, but White leaves his Queen in the line of fire and instead strikes with 16. Nxf7. GM Denker understands that with so many pieces in play he can sacrifice even his Queen for ... checkmate! Watch.

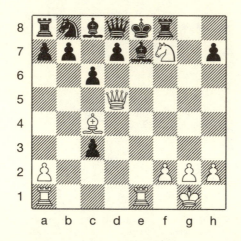

DIAGRAM 172

13. Since his game is lost, Black opts for the false glory of winning White's Queen by 16. ... cxd5. Black's alternative was the less sensational 16. ... Qb6(or c7) 17. Rxe7+ Kxe7 18. Re1+ Kf6 19. Qg5 mate. Notice how Black failed to develop his Queenside pieces. A preachment.

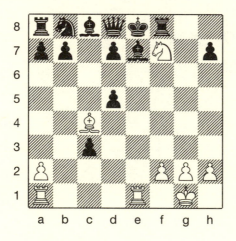

DIAGRAM 173

14. Here is the true glory: 17. Nd6 mate.

Throughout this game, Black's pieces were like moles in a hole, while White posted his forces directly in the center of the board and then lasered them at the opponent's King. An example of how quickly a game can be won because of opening play.

6 Chessercizes for Healthy Openings

THE GOOD NEWS ABOUT LEARNING how to play chess openings is that the major principles (centralization, rapid development and King safety) are nothing more than statements of simple common sense.

Of course, the devil is in the details. You must always temper adherence to principles with the demands of plain eyesight. If White begins a game with 1. f3? e5 2. g4??, Black must ignore the injunction against early Queen moves and play 2. ... Qh4 mate. If Black answers 1. e4 e5 2. Nc3 with the abominable 2. ... Ba3??, then White should forget for a moment about developing his pieces and play 3. bxa3, winning a piece.

What follows is a chess test that involves applying opening principles to specific positions and recognizing those instances when specifics override general principles. Examine the pieces in each diagram and then answer the questions to the side of the diagram. The answers are at the bottom of the page. If your answer is wrong or, still worse, if you fail to understand why it is wrong, then review the relevant portion of Chapter 5.

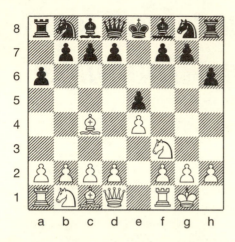

DIAGRAM 174

1. Which side has followed the "do's" of opening play?

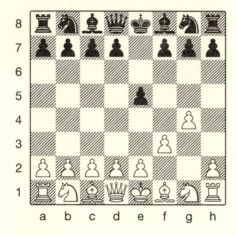

DIAGRAM 175

2. By playing 2. ... Qh4 mate, does Black violate the principle of not moving the Queen before developing the minor pieces?

ANSWERS

1. White is the good boy. He has developed two minor pieces and castled his King. Black has no pieces developed and has wasted time playing moves such as 2. ... a6 and 3. ... h6.

2. In a formal sense, yes. But the rule against developing the Queen before the minor pieces is based on the assumption that the opponent will make reasonable moves. In this instance, White played 1. f3? (opening his King and depriving the King Knight of the valuable f3 square) 1. ... e5 2. g4??, which allowed 2. ... Qh4 mate. Among chessplayers, this disaster is known as Fool's Mate and constitutes the shortest possible loss by checkmate.

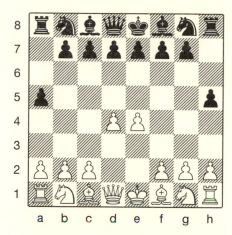

DIAGRAM 176

3. Can Black reasonably hope to develop his Rooks to a6 and h6? Is 3. c4 a bad move for White?

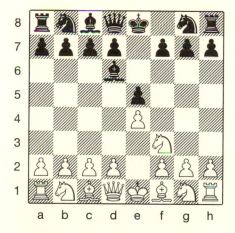

DIAGRAM 177

4. Black has just played 2. ... Bd6. Is the move good or bad?

ANSWERS

3. No, because White's Bishops cover a6 and h6. Black does not want to trade a Rook (5 points) for a Bishop (3 points). The move 3. c4 is not bad, as it helps to control the central d5 square. But quick development by 3. Nf3 and 4. Bc4 would give White a chance to cash in immediately on Black's neglect of the center. Among other things, White might eventually threaten Ng5 and Bxf7 mate.

4. Bad. Black wishes to protect the e-pawn from capture, but a better way to do so is 2. ... Nc6, developing a Knight before a Bishop. More importantly, 2. ... Bd6 congests Black's position by blocking in the d-pawn and preventing the freeing of the c8-h3 diagonal for the Queen Bishop. You must learn to plan ahead so that the negative features of a move like 2. ... Bd6 will be evident.

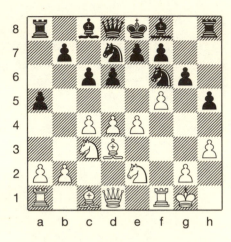

DIAGRAM 178

5. This position could have developed from Chessercize 3. Which side stands better?

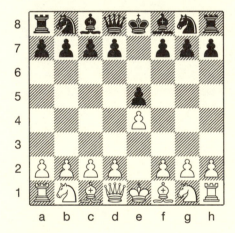

DIAGRAM 179

6. Would 2. d3 be a mistake?

ANSWERS

5. White does. He has made good on his control of the center, and his position—pawns in the middle of the board, pieces in the center, King castled—resembles a bulldozer about to push right through Black's midriff. His immediate threat is simply 1. fxg6 fxg6 2. e5 Ng8 3. Bxg6 mate.

6. Yes, though a very small one. The move 2. d3 opens the c1-h6 diagonal for White's Queen Bishop, but it also closes the f1-a6 diagonal for the King Bishop. True enough, White can still fianchetto his King Bishop, which is why 2. d3 is only a minor error. White does better to play 2. Nf3, 3. Bc4 and only later a possible d2-d3.

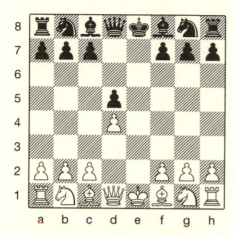

DIAGRAM 180

7. After 1. e4 e6 (the French Defense) 2. d4 d5.3. exd5 exd5, which side stands better?

DIAGRAM 181

8. Have both sides played reasonable opening moves?

ANSWERS

7. The position is close to even, with White still enjoying the advantage of moving first. Both sides have pawns in the center and open lines for Bishops and Queens.

8. Yes. This position is an example of hypermodernism discussed on page 108. The Bishops at g2 and g7 may not physically occupy the center, but they influence it from their flank positions on g2 and g7.

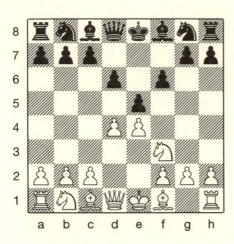

DIAGRAM 182

9. What is wrong with 4. Bd2?

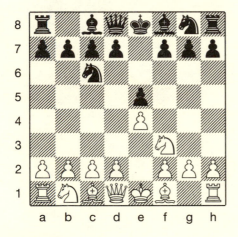

DIAGRAM 183

10. Is 3. Bd3 a good move?

ANSWERS

9. The problem with 4. Bd2 is not that it ruins White's position but that it fails to challenge Black's mistaken 3. ... f6 as vigorously as 4. Bc4. In addition, this Bishop move blocks in the White Queen. The Bishop would be better posted on e3 at some point.

10. No. True enough, 3. Bd3 does develop a piece and clear the way for White to castle. But either 3. Bc4 or 3. Bb5 gives the Bishop more scope and avoids blocking the d-pawn. Notice how White's Bishop on c1 is hemmed in. In truth, 3. Bd3 is a bit constipating.

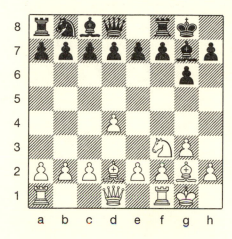

DIAGRAM 184

11. After 1. d4 Nf6 2. Nf3 g6 3. g3 Bg7 4. Bg2 0-0 5. 0-0 Ne4 6. Nbd2 Nxd2 7. Bxd2, White has an obvious lead in development. What principle did Black violate?

DIAGRAM 185

12. After 1. e4 e5 2. d4 exd4 3. c3 dxc3 4. Bc4 cxb2 5. Bxb2 Bb4+ 6. Nbd2 Qg5 7. Nf3, is 7. ... Qxg2 a bad move?

ANSWERS

11. Black moved a single piece—his King Knight—three times in the first six moves! Notice that after making two moves with the Knight, Black then traded it, leaving him with nothing to show for his three Knight moves. A better idea for Black was 6. ... d5, trying to anchor the Knight in the center.

12. Black is up two pawns, having spent his time snipping buttons while White was developing his pieces. Capturing the pawn on g2 only permits White to continue developing pieces while chasing the Queen around. The best move is 7. ... Bxd2+, though White's huge lead in development compensates him for being two pawns in arrears.

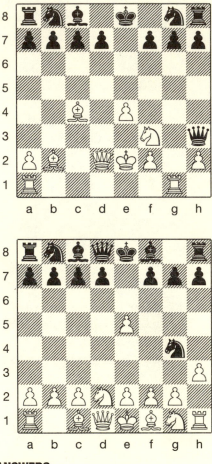

DIAGRAM 186

13. Black is three pawns ahead in material. Has he outplayed White in the opening?

DIAGRAM 187

14. After 1. d4 Nf6 2. Nd2 e5 3. dxe5 Ng4, White played 4. h3. Is this pawn move a violation of opening principles? Can Black prove it?

ANSWERS

13. No way! White has five of his six pieces developed, whereas among all of Black's pieces, only the Queen has moved from its original square. In this position (which is a continuation of the action in Chessercize 12), Black tried to develop with 10. ... Nf6 but got cut down after 11. Bxf7+ Kd8 (if 11. ... Kxf7, then White wins the Queen with 12. Ng5+) 12. Rxg7 Nxe4 (notice how Black is trying to carry out an attack with only two pieces developed) 13. Qg5+ Nxg5 14. Bf6 mate. See "The Evils of Pawn-Grubbing" on page 112.   *! check*

14. Yes on both counts. The move 4. h3 develops nothing and controls no important squares. In addition, it weakens the White King in an interesting way, for Black now plays 4. ... Ne3, attacking White's Queen. If 5. fxe3, then Black has 5. ... Qh4+ 6. g3 Qxg3 mate. A better move for White is 4. Ngf3, developing toward the center.

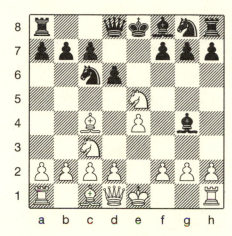

DIAGRAM 188

15. After 1. e4 e5 2. Nf3 d6 3. Bc4 Nc6 4. Nc3 Bg4 5. Nxe5??, Black played 5. ... Bxd1. What opening principles does this move violate? Can White punish Black?

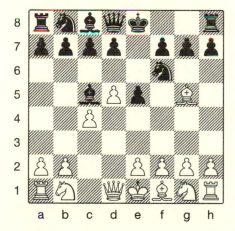

DIAGRAM 189

16. After 1. d4 Nf6 2. c4 e5 3. d5 Bc5, White just played 4. Bg5. Who stands better? Does Black have a good move?

ANSWERS

15. Up to the position shown in the diagram, Black has played a good game. Black can now win a Queen by 5. ... Bxd1, but this violates the imperative of maintaining King safety. White wins the game by 6. Bxf7+ Ke7 7. Nd5 mate. Instead, Black can be happy winning the Knight with 5. ... Nxe5, and suddenly White's little trick backfires.

16. White's 4. Bg5 is an unhappy thought that violates three opening principles: (1) moving a Queenside piece before Kingside ones; (2) moving a Bishop before an available Knight (correct was 4. Nf3); and most importantly, (3) putting White's King in jeopardy. Black can now play 4. ... Ne4, threatening 5. ... Bxf2 mate. White's best chance is 5. Be3, though Black has a winning position after 5. ... Bxe3 6. fxe3 Qh4+ 7. g3 Nxg3 8. Nf3 Qh6.

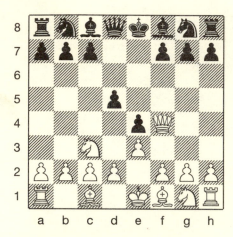

DIAGRAM 190

17. After 1. e3 e5 2. Qf3? d5 3. Nc3 e4 4. Qf4?, how does Black punish White's premature development of his Queen?

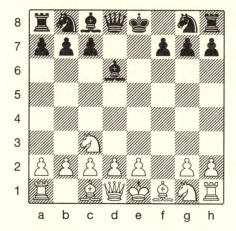

DIAGRAM 191

18. After 1. f4 e5 2. fxe5 d6 3. exd6 Bxd6 4. Nc3, how does Black force mate?

ANSWERS

17. The best move for Black is 4. ... Bd6, trapping the White lady in an open field. The Queen has no safe move.

18. White's f-pawn is gone, and he now pays the penalty after 4. ... Qh4+ 5. g3 Qxg3+ (or 5. ... Bxg3+) 6. hxg3 Bxg3 mate. Moving the f-pawn in the opening is extremely risky and must, therefore, be very carefully considered.

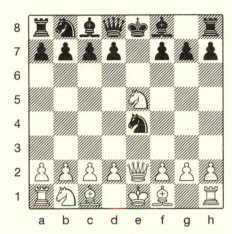

DIAGRAM 192

19. After 1. e4 e5 2. Nf3 Nf6 (Petroff's Defense) 3. Nxe5 Nxe4? (better is 3. ... d6) 4. Qe2, what happens if Black plays 4. ... Nf6?

DIAGRAM 193

20. After 1. e4 c5 (the Sicilian Defense) 2. Nf3 d6 3. d4 cxd4 4. Nxd4 Nf6 5. Nc3 g6 6. Bc4 Nc6? (correct is Kingside development with 6. ... Bg7) 7. Nxc6 bxc6 8. e5, should Black play 8. .... dxe5?

ANSWERS

19. After 4. ... Nf6, White wins Black's Queen by 5. Nc6+ Qe7 6. Nxe7. Or if 5. ... Be7, then 6. Nxd8.

20. No. After 8. ... dxe5, White plays 9. Bxf7+ Kxf7 10. Qxd8, winning the Queen. Relatively best is 8. ... Ng4, when Black has a bad but not totally lost game. Were Black's Bishop already on g7 by some chance, then the Black Queen would not be lost because the King Rook could recapture White's Queen.

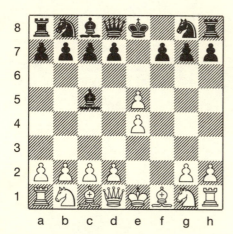

DIAGRAM 194

21. After 1. e4 e5 2. f4 Bc5 (the King's Gambit Declined) 3. fxe5??, how does Black exploit White's weakening of his King?

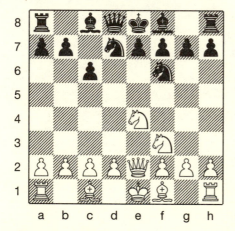

DIAGRAM 195

22. This position arises after 1. e4 c6 (the Caro-Kann Defense) 2. Nc3 d5 3. Nf3 dxe4 4. Nxe4 Nd7 5. Qe2 Ngf6. What is White's best move?

ANSWERS

21. The move is 3. ... Qh4+. After 4. Ke2, the end is 4. ... Qxe4 mate. And on 4. g3, Black wins a Rook by 4. ... Qxe4+ and 5. ... Qxh1.

22. White's horse delivers the knockout kick by 6. Nd6 mate. Black neglected King safety. Instead, a move such as 5. ... e6 would be quite playable.

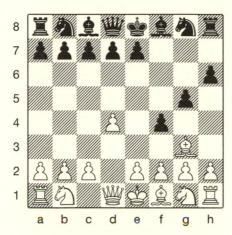

DIAGRAM 196

23. After 1. d4 f5 (the Dutch Defense) 2. Bg5 h6 3. Bh4 g5 4. Bg3 f4?, how does White avoid the loss of his Bishop and exploit Black's weakening of his King?

DIAGRAM 197

24. From Chessercize 23, play continued 5. e3 h5 6. Bd3 Rh6? (better is 6. ... e5). How can White checkmate in two moves?

ANSWERS

23. Black wildly advanced his Kingside pawns, leaving a lot of light squares open around his King. The correct move is 5. e3, threatening 6. Qh5 mate. See the next diagram for the final chapter of this serial.

24. The two-move stunner is 7. Qxh5+ Rxh5 (if 7. ... Rg6, then 8. Qxg6 mate) 8. Bg6 mate.

7 *Middlegame Strategy & Tactics*

THE MIDDLEGAME IS THE PORTION of the chess battle between the opening and the endgame. In most games, the middlegame begins about move 15 and runs through move 35, although there are specific openings such as the Exchange Variation of the Ruy Lopez (see page 232) in which pieces are traded very quickly and the ending itself begins on move 10!

If the opening is the building phase during which the two players create a position with distinct features, and if the endgame is the moment to exploit reasonably permanent advantages or to hang on for dear life, then the middlegame is the planning phase. These are, of course, approximate descriptions if only because players often find themselves hanging on for dear life in the middlegame and doing a lot of planning in the endgame. Still, the complications of the middlegame can be so rich that unexpected developments cause even grandmasters constantly to revise existing plans or plot new ones.

So important is planning that Emanuel Lasker, world champion from 1894 to 1921, argued quite seriously that it is better to play with a bad plan than with no plan at all.

THE CONCEPT OF PLANNING

Like life itself, a chess game contains many moments when a player must select a course of action to best exploit the potential of his position. The task is to overcome obstacles to reach a specific goal—be it winning the game by trading off pieces when enjoying an advantage in material or holding a draw in a bad position.

Let's look at a real-life position in which White must formulate a plan. A brief glance at the position in Diagram 198 shows that although material is even, White obviously stands better. His pieces are all attacking weak spots in the Black position (the pawns on b7 and especially on d5), while Black's two Rooks and Bishop are engaged strictly in defending them. As for Black's Queen, this piece is stuck on f8 where it attacks and defends nothing.

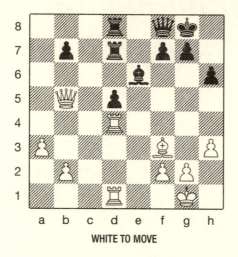

DIAGRAM 198

WHITE TO MOVE

When formulating a plan in chess, there is a time-tested order in thinking that is called the ***analytical method***, which can be applied to the above position as follows:

1. Begin by thinking defensively. Does Black's last move (1. ... Rad8) threaten me in any way? If so, how do I deal with the threat? It is impossible to overestimate the importance of initial defensive thinking in the analytical method. The answer is that 1. ... Rad8 is clearly a defensive move meant to shore up protection of the d-pawn and does not contain a threat.

2. Look around the board. Are your pieces under attack and, if so, are they adequately defended? True enough, in the above position, Black's last move threatened nothing, but there is always the chance that both you and the opponent overlooked a possibility that could have been played the previous move and may now be played the next move. Still, the answer here is that none of White's pieces are under attack.

3. Cast an eye to your King. Does it remain safe? The most heartbreaking thing in chess is to outplay an opponent completely, win a couple of pieces, and then toss away the game because of a single careless move. Later in this chapter, you will study back-rank mates, which are administered by a Queen or Rook on either the first or eighth rank and which are often the result of one side moving quickly without ensuring King safety. The answer here is that White's King is safe and even enjoys an escape hatch on h2. (When you have castled Kingside, we recommend playing h2-h3 as White or ... h7-h6 as Black at a suitable point in the middlegame to increase King safety.)

4. Additional steps in the analytical method are given in the box on page 161. Regarding the position in Diagram 198, the next relevant question for White to ask is whether Black has any piece or pawn that can be captured for free or any weakness that can be exploited. There are no free Black pieces or pawns ripe for the picking, but the *isolated pawn* on d5—an isolated pawn is one without friendly pawns that can defend it from adjacent files—is obviously under attack and therefore constitutes a weakness. Before looking further at how to exploit this weakness at d5, White may also look quickly at Black's pawn on b7 (attacked only by the Queen and defended by the Black Rook) and at Black's King (no White pieces are currently directed at the King, and the powerful White Queen is on the other side of the board with no easy way to reach the Kingside). Clearly, neither of these options is as attractive as concentrating on winning the attacked d-pawn.

Fine. Having concluded that the d-pawn is the relevant weakness, White needs to formulate a plan for its capture. Here is how a practiced player would think: "Okay, I'm attacking it four times, and he is defending it only three times. Now let's check the value of the attackers and defenders. I have two Rooks and a Bishop attacking the pawn, and he also has two Rooks and a Bishop defending it. But in addition, I have my Queen hitting the pawn, and, what's more important, I can use the Queen to make the final capture and net a pawn." A plan is thus born, and the following captures occur:

1.	Bxd5	Bxd5
2.	Rxd5	Rxd5
3.	Rxd5	Rxd5
4.	Qxd5	

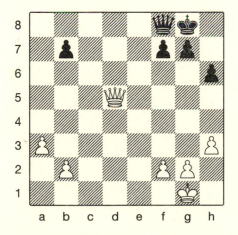

DIAGRAM 199

White is up a pawn in a Queen-and-pawn endgame. With best play, White ought to win, though Black has fighting chances to hold on.

And what happens next? A new situation—an endgame—has arisen, and the analytical method is again employed by both sides:

- White will identify Black's weaknesses and formulate a plan to win the game (most likely, he will advance his Queenside pawns to create a *passed pawn*—a pawn that has no enemy pawn in front of it or on immediately adjacent files—and then usher it to the eighth rank to make a second Queen with the intention of arraying this superior fire-power against the Black King).

- Black will look for opportunities to hold a draw by regaining his lost pawn or delivering perpetual check on the White King.

EXPLOITING A MATERIAL ADVANTAGE

In a battle between relative beginners, the most common problem to solve at some point in the middlegame is how to exploit a material advantage. Two methods can be recommended:

- Exchange pieces and transpose into a winning endgame.

- Use one's superior force to attack the enemy King.

The decision to exchange pieces in order to enter an endgame rests on whether the material advantage is likely to be decisive. Can the opponent prevent progress after pieces are traded and keep the position blocked? Is the resulting endgame likely to come down to King + Bishop versus King or King + Knight versus King, both of which are forced draws because the stronger side is unable to force mate no matter how poorly the weaker side may play? A hint: Try to keep at least one pawn that can later become a Queen.

Another approach, which is sometimes speedier, is to explore any weaknesses in the placement of the enemy King. In Diagram 200 from the late middlegame, White is up a pawn and can now choose between trading off Queens and Rooks or trying to make use of the Bishop that rakes the a1-h8 diagonal leading to the Black King.

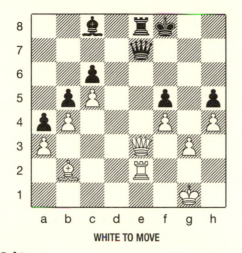

DIAGRAM 200

WHITE TO MOVE

1.   **Qd4**

Using the analytical method, White immediately investigates whether Black's last move (... Be6-c8) contains a threat. It does. With 1. ... Qxe3+ 2. Rxe3 Rxe3, Black wins a Rook. In this simplified position with an extra Rook, Black will win easily; White need not concern himself with such further questions as King safety, since his monarch will inevitably suffer the worst.

White must now look at how to parry the threatened loss of a Rook, and two ideas come to mind: He can either trade off Queens and Rooks by a series of captures on e7 and hope to win the ending with his extra pawn, or he can move the Queen to c3 or d4, uncovering his Rook on Black's Queen, and then attack the Black King along the long, dark-squared diagonal. If Black captures the Rook, then White plays Qg7 mate.

The possible endgame occurs after 1. Qxe7+ Rxe7 2. Rxe7 Kxe7. Further moves might be 3. Kf2 Ke6 4. Ke3 Bd7. White's problem is that his dark-squared Bishop can attack none of Black's pawns on light squares. Still worse, White's King is unable to penetrate Black's side of the board. Clearly, the second player can now shift his Bishop back and forth between, say, d7 and e8 *ad infinitum*. The game is a draw despite White's extra pawn.

Still, White now knows that he has a draw at the very worst, and he loses nothing by exploring the option of attacking Black's King, which he eventually chooses to do. After all, White's Bishop is clearly superior to Black's cleric, which is hemmed in by its own pawns. Chess is a game of logic, and it is logical that the player with extra material and more actively posted pieces should be able to capitalize on this superiority.

In this position, either 1. Qd4 or 1. Qc3 wins quickly.

1.   **...**   **Qh7**

The only move. On 1. ... Be6, White has 2. Rxe6 Qxe6 3. Qg7 mate. Other tries are 1. ... Qd7 2. Qh8+ Kf7 3. Qg7 mate (notice how White's Rook prevents the escape of the enemy King) and 1. ... Qf7 2. Qh8+ Qg8 3. Rxe8+ Kxe8 4. Qxg8+, finishing up a full Queen.

2.	Qf6+	Qf7

Once again, the defense is forced. On 2. ... Kg8, White has 3. Rxe8 mate.

3.	Qh8+	Qg8
4.	Rxe8+	Kxe8
5.	Qxg8+	

White is up a Queen. His decision to use his material and positional advantage by attacking the Black King was clearly correct in this position. However, there are many other positions where either trading pieces or attacking the King works equally well.

ELEMENTS OF MIDDLEGAME STRATEGY

In chess, strategy refers to general and long-range planning, which concerns what must be done to achieve a certain goal. We have already discussed the analytical method that should be applied when formulating plans or strategy.

Key elements to consider when plotting strategy—that is, making a plan—are force, space and time, though these factors must always be viewed in light of the overall position, which includes, as we will discuss, King safety. "You may be behind in Force or Material," former world champion Jose Capablanca wrote in his *Primer of Chess*, "and yet have a winning position. You may be behind in Time and yet have a winning position. You may be behind in Space and yet have a winning position. And finally you may be behind in all three of the elements, Material, Space, and Time, and yet have a winning position." Capablanca's point is not that force, space and time are unimportant; indeed, he regards them as critical when considering middlegame strategy. His point is to avoid mechanistic thinking when applying these concepts.

Force is a general term for the amount of material at your disposal. If you have a Queen (9 points), two Rooks (10 points) and a Bishop (3 points), then measured in point value, you have 22 points of force. If you see a possibility to leave the opponent with only 17 points, then your strategy is directed toward gaining the equivalent of a Rook (5 points).

This kind of calculation of force is very crude. We saw in the Denker–Shayne chess movie given in Chapter 5 that White was well behind in material but that what counted was his local superiority on the front near

Black's King. Diagram 201 shows a stunning example of a force imbalance overwhelmingly in White's favor, yet it is Black, world champion Garry Kasparov, who is winning.

JAIME SUNYE-NETO–GARRY KASPAROV
GRAZ, 1981

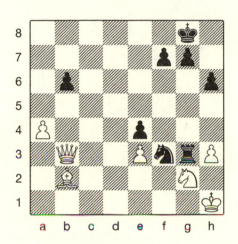

DIAGRAM 201

Black's threat in this position (which did not actually occur in the game, but represents one possible outcome) is simply 1. ... Rxh3 mate. If White tries to create an escape route for his King by moving his Knight to any square, then Black finishes with 1. ... Rg1 mate. Known as the Arabian Knight mate, this effective cooperation of Rook with Knight to mate the King is examined later in this chapter.

The importance of force in chess goes beyond simple counting of points; a lot depends on who enjoys local superiority in force where the crucial battle is being fought.

That's basic Napoleon—and basic chess.

Space can be defined as the amount of board territory that a player occupies, controls or influences. The pieces of the player with more space almost always have more mobility, which is the capacity to maneuver. The side whose pieces are huddled behind pawns, which themselves are not far advanced, possesses little if any mobility. In Diagram 202, material is even, and White's Bishop is even stymied from participating in the battle. Yet

White has such an advantage in space occupied, controlled and influenced that he has an easy win.

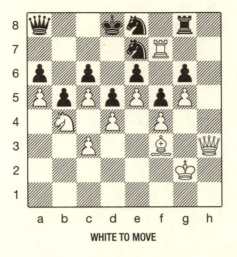

DIAGRAM 202

WHITE TO MOVE

The winning move is 1. Qh7, threatening 2. Rxe7 and 3. Qxg8. So constricted is Black that he has nowhere to shift his Rook and has no useful Knight moves (compared with White's steed on b4, which is bearing down on a6 and c6). A possible defense with 1. ... Qb7 is answered crushingly by 2. Rxe7 Qxe7 3. Nxc6+, winning the Queen and mating soon. Another discombobulating move is 3. Qxg8.

Not all spatial advantages are as optically obvious as in Diagram 202. But a sure sign that one side is cramped is when his pieces are huddled together on a few contiguous squares and are sitting behind pawns that have nowhere to go.

Time refers to the making of a move that has developmental value. Chess people speak of "losing time" when a player retreats a piece to its previous square without good reason or simply makes inconsequential moves. In the opening, Black is said to have lost considerable time after 1. e4 h6 2. d4 a6—about two *tempos*, which can be defined as the time or value represented by a move. When compared with White's two pawn moves, which occupy important central squares and open up lines for White's Queen and two Bishops, Black's puny pawn pushes on the edge of the board have little value.

Loss of time in the middlegame is usually the result of failing to make a plan and of shifting pieces aimlessly. In Diagram 203, both sides are equal in force. White's two extra pawns are offset by Black having a Rook and two Knights against the Queen. Yet in terms of space and time, White enjoys a decisive advantage.

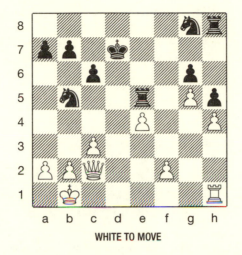

DIAGRAM 203

WHITE TO MOVE

Black's problem obviously lies in his undeveloped Kingside pieces and in the fact that they are constricted in their mobility. The Knight on g8 can safely go only to e7, when any further forward advance is blocked by White's e-pawn, which controls both d5 and f5. As for the Rook on h8, its only opportunity to enter the fray is by relocating to the f-file. White, on the other hand, can mobilize his Queen and Rook immediately along the open d-file and launch an attack on the Black monarch.

1.	Rd1+	Kc8

White loses no time whatsoever by grabbing the open file with his Rook. Occupying open files with Rooks, like grabbing open diagonals for Bishops or hopping Knights toward the center, is usually sound middlegame strategy. Whenever in doubt as to what to do and when there is an open file at hand, then occupy it with a Rook or Queen. All other factors being equal, you seldom go far wrong by increasing the scope of your pieces.

Let's assume for the moment that White did not play this position vigorously and instead settled upon the line 1. a3 Ne7 2. Ka2 Re8 3. b3 Nc8 4. f3. Suddenly Black is back in the game because White has "lost time" with pointless moves, while Black has managed to mobilize both of his Kingside pieces, thereby "gaining time."

2.	Qd2	Ne7

White threatened 3. Qd8 mate. Notice that in addition to grabbing the open d-file with his Rook, White also places his Queen in front of the Rook, thereby doubling on the file and taking complete control of this central line. In most games, the only thing better than occupying an open file with a Rook is to double Rooks or a Rook and Queen on that file.

3.	Qd7+	Kb8
4.	a4	Nc7
5.	Qd4	**Black resigns**

White's last move skewers Black's Rooks; if the attacked Rook on e5 moves, White plays Qxh8. This major tactical theme is discussed later in the chapter.

KING SAFETY

A constant theme throughout this book is the importance of early castling, usually on the Kingside, in order to slide the monarch out of harm's way. If in the opening King safety is advisable, and if in the endgame it is an occasional concern (even with pared-down forces), then in the middlegame it is an absolute must that is fully on a par with force, space and time.

Diagram 204 and Diagram 205 offer a tale of two centralized Kings—the first in the endgame, the second in the middlegame.

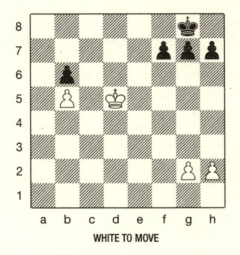

DIAGRAM 204

WHITE TO MOVE

The vicissitudes of struggle have left White in Diagram 204 with his King smack-dab in the center at d5, while Black's castled monarch has remained safely behind his undisturbed pawns. The second player is even up a pawn, but White will be an easy winner because a centralized King is a strong King when there are no enemy forces to attack it. Never forget: The King also has fighting power.

White played 1. Kc6, whereupon Black gave up. Two possible lines are 1. ... Kf8 2. Kxb6 Ke7 3. Kc7, followed by 4. b6, 5. b7 and 6. b8=Q; and 1. ... f5 2. Kxb6 g5 3. Kc7 f4 4. b6 g4 5. b7 and 6. b8=Q+. In both instances, White scores effortlessly.

Compare the happy fate of the centralized endgame King with this beheading of a centralized middlegame King:

WEINSTEIN–ROMERO
MENDOZA, 1932

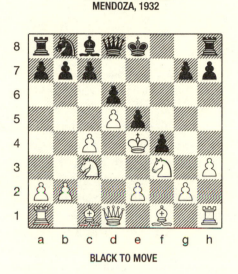

DIAGRAM 205

BLACK TO MOVE

White enjoys a huge advantage in both force (an extra Bishop and Knight) and time (Black has no pieces developed, whereas White has both Knights out). Yet so great is White's disadvantage in King safety that Black quickly finishes off the game by 1. ... Bf5+ 2. Kxf5 Qf6+ 3. Ke4 Qg6 mate. If White varies with 3. Kg4, then Black plays 3. ... h5 mate.

The key elements of middlegame strategy—force, space, time and King safety—boil down to seven practical commandments:

1. Create, maintain and increase piece mobility.

2. Treat central control not merely as an end in itself. Be prepared to strike out from the center into the enemy position, including into corners where the King lurks.

3. Grab open files for Rooks and Queens.

4. Put Bishops on open diagonals—and the longer the diagonal, usually the better.

5. Maneuver Knights in or near the center.

6. Keep the King out of harm's way behind a wall of pawns, usually by castling early on the Kingside. Move the pawns in front of the King only for compelling reasons.

7. Get the Queen into the middle of the fight. (However, in the opening phase, usually keep the Queen at home unless there is a compelling reason otherwise, such as a winning attack.)

TACTICAL THEMES

If strategy deals with what must be done during a game to reach a given goal, then tactics deal with how to execute a plan or strategy. Tactics are often implemented by playing *combinations*, which are forced variations of moves designed to achieve a definite aim. Combinations frequently contain a *sacrifice*—a voluntary surrender of material for some hoped-for advantage. The goal of a combination may be to checkmate the enemy King, to win material, to procure a draw in an inferior position, and so forth. The interior content of a combination—the sequence of moves—contains tactical themes or devices, which are tactical ideas that occur again and again in chess games.

Three of the most common tactical devices are pins, double attacks and skewers.

The most common of the three is the *pin*, which makes an appearance in virtually every chess game. A pin occurs when three men stand in a line on a diagonal, rank or file. The pinned man (any piece or pawn except the King) stands in the middle, and the shielded man (usually a piece of greater value than the pinned man) stands behind this middle piece. The pinning piece (a Queen, Rook or Bishop) is part of the enemy's force and stands in front of the middle piece. In Diagram 206, White's Rook on g2 is the pinned man, the King on h1 the shielded man, and the enemy Bishop on f3 the pinning piece.

DIAGRAM 206

BLACK TO MOVE

Thanks to the ***absolute pin*** of the Rook on g2—a pin in which the pinned man cannot legally move because the shielded man is the King—Black can now play 1. ... Rh3 mate!

Here is a ***relative pin:***

GARRY KASPAROV–GREG HJORTH
DORTMUND, 1980

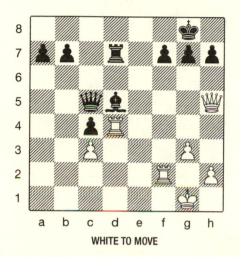

DIAGRAM 207

WHITE TO MOVE

The future world champion now played 1. Rf5, pinning Black's Bishop on his Queen. Hjorth resigned because the Bishop is lost, being attacked three times and defended only twice. Still, Black could legally move the Bishop and surrender his far more valuable Queen, which makes the pin relative.

The prevalence and importance of pins in the royal game has led chess wags to say lamentable things such as the pin is mightier than the sword or, still worse, the pin is mightier than the swordfish.

A ***double attack*** occurs when a piece or pawn simultaneously attacks two enemy men or attacks, say, one enemy man and contains a deadly threat elsewhere on the board. In the game between Boris Spassky, the world champion from 1969 to 1972, and Russian master Oleg Averkin, Spassky as White played a devastating double attack:

BORIS SPASSKY–OLEG AVERKIN
MOSCOW, 1973

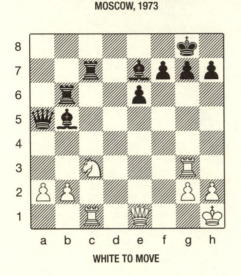

DIAGRAM 208

WHITE TO MOVE

Spassky's killer move was 1. Qe5, which threatens to capture the Black Rook on c7 and to checkmate on g7. Black must guard against the mate, and when he does, the Rook on c7 goes. Note that on 1. ... Bf6, White can play 2. Qxf6 because the g-pawn is pinned on the Black King; if 2. ... g6, then 3. Qd8+, picking up the Rook in addition to the Bishop.

The Spassky–Averkin position is doubly instructive because the position immediately preceding Diagram 208 featured a pinning combination that led to the double attack:

BORIS SPASSKY–OLEG AVERKIN

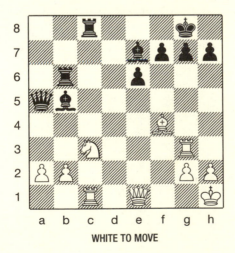

DIAGRAM 209

WHITE TO MOVE

This position occurred only one move before the preceding example and is an illustration of how two tactical devices—pinning and double attack—come together to form a short two-move combination. Every combination has three elements:

- **Situation**—a position that warns us, "Beware, a combination might be possible!"

- **Idea**—the tactical devices, in this case pinning and double attack, used to carry out the combination.

- **Goal**—the desired result of winning a piece, checkmating and so on.

Of course, when mulling over a combination, you should follow the steps of the analytical method. But combinations contain an additional imperative: Before launching one, you must have a clear picture of the final position in mind.

Spassky won from Diagram 209 as follows: 1. Bc7 (pinning the Rook on the Queen and threatening to win a Rook for a Bishop) 1. ... Rxc7 (relieving the pin by capturing the Bishop) 2. Qe5 (a double attack). Spassky saw that the situation with Black's pieces scrunched together on the Queenside was unusual. He then saw two tactical devices, a pin and a double attack, that seemed to win material. And he clearly visualized the final position that wins a Rook for a Bishop.

Like pins, a *skewer* involves three pieces, and it has been described as a reverse pin. Our name for it is the "shish-kebab" tactic. Diagram 210 shows a very simple skewer:

DIAGRAM 210

In a pin, the object is to hold the middle piece in place or to gain an advantage if it moves; in a skewer, the object is to force the middle piece to move so that the piece behind it is exposed to capture. Thus, the White

Bishop checks the Black King, forcing it to move and exposing the Black Rook to capture. Skewers are delivered by Queens, Rooks and Bishops.

Diagram 211 shows a short two-move combination involving an attack followed by a skewer:

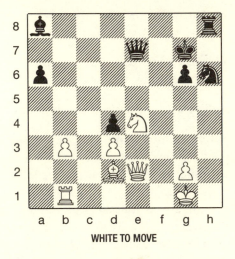

DIAGRAM 211

WHITE TO MOVE

Do you see the trick? White wins a Rook for a Bishop by 1. Bg5 Qe6 (other Queen moves are also inadequate) 2. Bf6+ Kg8 3. Bxh8.

In top-flight professional chess, games are seldom won by employing a single tactical device during a game. For one grandmaster to defeat another, he must usually employ a variety of strategical and tactical weapons. In Diagram 212, world-champion-to-be Garry Kasparov tests his steel against Grandmaster Lev Alburt, one of the authors of this book. To win this game, Kasparov employs or threatens to employ all three of the tactical devices discussed in this chapter and a fourth besides.

LEV ALBURT–GARRY KASPAROV
LUCERNE, 1982

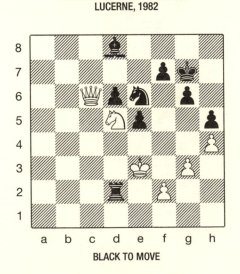

DIAGRAM 212

BLACK TO MOVE

1.	...	Re2+!

This decoy sacrifice is designed to lure the White King to e2 by letting White capture the unprotected Rook. If 2. Kxe2, Black has 2. ... Nd4+, *forking* or double-attacking White's King and Queen. Hence...

2.	Kd3	e4+
3.	Kc4	Rc2+

"Shish kebab!" Black plays a skewer on the King and Queen, forcing White into a ...

4.	Nc3	

... pin. Notice that Black's Rook on c2 now pins the Knight on White's King.

4.	...	Bf6

Black attacks the pinned Knight twice, and White has no good defense. Using a myriad of tactical devices, Kasparov has beautifully created a position where he will gain a decisive advantage in force or material. What follows is the mopping up operation.

5.	Qxe4	Rxc3+
6.	Kd5	Rc5+
7.	Kxd6	Be5+

White resigns

White can now see the inevitable conclusion: 8. Kd7 Rc7+ 9. Ke8 Bd6, threatening 10. ... Re7 mate. The cooperation of Rook, Bishop and Knight in this mate constitutes a mating pattern seen occasionally in over-the-board play.

Now it's time to deal with several of the more common mating patterns, including a couple that are related to those employed by Kasparov against Alburt.

THE MATING GAME

The central fact of chess life is that checkmate is the name of the game. You may enjoy huge advantages in force, space and time and still lose if the apparently weaker side contrives to place your King in checkmate.

The role of luck in chess is confined to freak events (floods and power outages stopping games) and mortality, though even in this event there can be unexpected equalizing justice. On one—and only one—occasion (in the mid-1930s), Dutch master Dr. Adolf Olland was enjoying what chess people call a "dead won" position when he also dropped dead of a heart attack right at the chessboard.

Bad luck indeed. But his opponent then chivalrously resigned the game, proving that even in dire circumstances chess results are mainly based not on cosmic tampering but on performance.

Mating positions, for example, are not unique events that leap at the losing party without warning. There are several well-known mating patterns that occur repeatedly, albeit in different overall settings.

Among beginners, one of the most common patterns is called the **back-rank mate.** We call it the "heartbreak mate," because this particular checkmate often bedevils the side that is otherwise ahead, turning a win into a loss with a single careless move. In Diagram 213, White has just played 1. Rc1-c3, with the idea of capturing Black's g3 pawn.

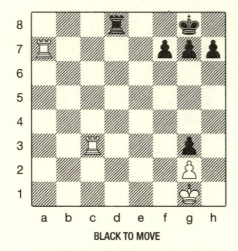

DIAGRAM 213

BLACK TO MOVE

Black, who was dead lost until White's astonishing blunder, responds with 1. ... Rd1 mate. Notice how Black's g3-pawn guards the potential escape squares of f2 and h2. Instead, White could have won easily by 1. Rca1, with the unstoppable threat of 2. Ra8, trading Rooks. Or, for that matter, by 1. Ra3.

Here is another example in which White is up two Bishops:

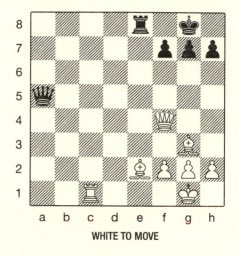

DIAGRAM 214

WHITE TO MOVE

White notices that Black is attacking the Bishop on e2 and decides to protect against the threat by 1. Bf3??, failing to notice the second threat of 1. ... Qe1+ 2. Rxe1 Rxe1 mate. Instead, White can save his Bishop and win the game effortlessly by 1. Bf1.

These kinds of back-rank mates are elementary, and the losing party in both cases would surely have seen them if he had taken a second look before leaping. As the old saying goes, "The game ain't over 'til the last man's out."

While back-rank mates are delivered by Rooks and Queens, they are frequently inflicted with the cooperation of other pieces. The Rook + Bishop pattern is seen frequently.

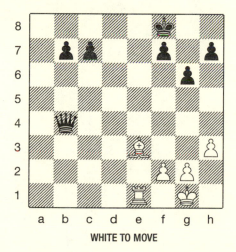

DIAGRAM 215

WHITE TO MOVE

White forces mate by 1. Bh6+ Kg8 2. Re8+ Qf8 3. Rxf8 mate.

A *smothered mate* is delivered by a solo Knight against a King that is generally blocked by its own pieces or pawns and has, therefore, no move. The classic pattern is given in Diagram 216.

DIAGRAM 216

WHITE TO MOVE

The smothering process begins with a check, 1. Nf7+ Kg8. It is followed by a double check, 2. Nh6+ Kh8 (remember: a King in double check must move, and on 2. ... Kf8, White plays 3. Qf7 mate). It is climaxed by a Queen sacrifice, 3. Qg8+ Rxg8. And it is consummated by the Knight, 4. Nf7 mate.

The *two-Knight mate* is often preceded by a decoy and/or obstruction sacrifice that forces an opposing piece to block a potential escape square for the enemy King:

DIAGRAM 217

WHITE TO MOVE

White begins with 1. Qg7+. This decoy sacrifice of the Queen forces Black to place his Rook on g7 with 1. ... Rxg7, which allows 2. Nh6 mate. The important point is that if there were no Black Rook on g7, then Nh6+ would be answered by ... Kg7. The stuff of Knightmares.

The *epaulette mate* is also known as the militant mate among chess wags, and it occurs when the victim King is blocked on the immediate left and right by its own men.

PAUL KERES–ROBERT FISCHER
BLED, 1959

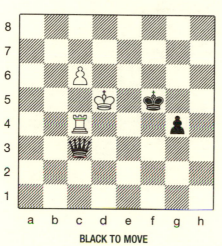

DIAGRAM 218

BLACK TO MOVE

Bobby Fischer was only 16 when he defeated the great Estonian grandmaster Paul Keres (1916–75) with 1. ... Qe5 mate. The White King is prevented from escaping because of the Rook on c4 and pawn on c6, which are suggestive of shoulder boards or epaulettes.

Two-Rook mates are self-explanatory: Two Rooks cooperate somewhere on the board, though usually along the edge, to checkmate the enemy King. The next position is from a game that was aptly dubbed a "Hollywood beauty," being played in Tinsel Town back in 1932. The victor, Alexander Alekhine, was world champion from 1927 to 1935 and later from 1937 until his death in 1946. He was famous for his flashy sacrifices, and here he pulls off a beauty even though playing blindfolded against the strong California master, Harry Borochow.

ALEXANDER ALEKHINE–HARRY BOROCHOW
HOLLYWOOD, 1932

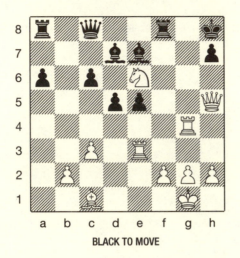

DIAGRAM 219

BLACK TO MOVE

White has just played 1. Ng7-e6, and Black chooses to resign. The problem is that after 1. ... Bxe6 or any other reasonable move, White plays 2. Qxh7+ Kxh7 3. Rh3+ Bh4 4. Rhxh4 mate. A classic two-Rook mate.

The *Arabian mate* features the cooperation of Rook and Knight to force checkmate. The Knight's role is to protect the Rook and to block a potential escape square for the enemy King; the Rook's job is to administer the mate. At the U.S. Open Championship of 1933, famous American Grandmaster Reuben Fine (1914–93) defeats Grandmaster Arthur Dake of Portland, Oregon, with a deadly Arabian mate. Do you see how?

REUBEN FINE–ARTHUR DAKE
DETROIT, 1933

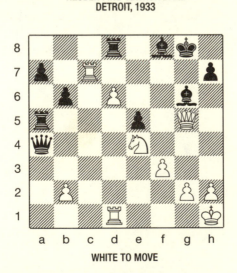

DIAGRAM 220

WHITE TO MOVE

Black is up a piece. But the issue is not who has more, but who has the mostest where it counts. Black threatens a back-rank mate with 1. ... Qxd1, but White lands the first punch with 1. Qxg6+ hxg6 2. Nf6+ Kh8 3. Rh7 mate. Chessplayers say that Arabian mates are meant for romantic Arabian knights.

THE ANALYTICAL METHOD IN CHESS THINKING

The analytical method provides a "reality check" as you contemplate your next move. You put yourself in a critical mindset, analyzing your opponent's move and your intended response against a checklist of simple questions designed to prevent you from making obvious errors. Before each move, ask yourself:

1. Does my opponent's last move contain a threat? If so, deal with it.

2. Are my own pieces all adequately protected? Has my opponent left a piece exposed to capture for free?

3. Is my King still safe? Is the opponent's King vulnerable? For example, is it possible to sacrifice a pawn to prevent the enemy King from castling?

4. Did my opponent meet the threat offered by my last move?

5. Do I still have pieces that need development?

6. Can I move a Rook to an open file—say, the d- or e-file? Is it possible to double Rooks or a Queen and Rook on a useful open file?

7. Does my opponent have a weakness that can be exploited?

8. If so, how can the weakness be exploited? (Find a way to exploit a weakness that involves making a plan!)

9. Does the move I plan to make overlook something very, very simple, such as the loss of a piece or checkmate? Train yourself to look around at the position "with the eyes of a beginner," as Russian players often say.

The analytical method isn't just for the middlegame. Use it to validate your opening and endgame play as well.

The two Bishops often cooperate in giving the *crisscross mate*, which is also termed the double-cross by surprised opponents.

OFSTAD–WOLFGANG UHLMANN
HALLE, 1963

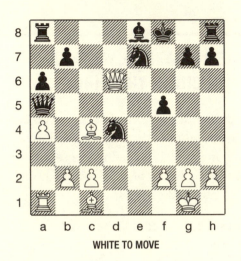

DIAGRAM 221

WHITE TO MOVE

The conclusion is 1. Qf6+ gxf6 2. Bh6 mate. White's two Bishops literally crisscross, with one guarding the light squares and the other the dark squares. Of course, the Queen could also be used to achieve this pattern by replacing one of the Bishops on either c4 or h6.

When a Knight and Bishop cooperate to deliver checkmate in the middlegame, they are usually working against a castled King position that has been weakened by the pawn move g2-g3 for White or ... g7-g6 for Black. Typically, though not always, the side suffering mate is without a fianchettoed Bishop on either g2 or g7. In the example of the Bishop and Knight mate in Diagram 222, Black has just played 1. ... Ne6-g5:

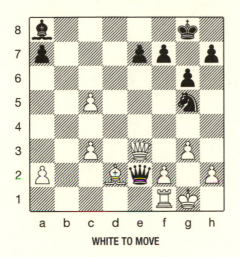

WOLFGANG UHLMANN–HEINZ LIEBERT
EAST GERMANY, 1976

DIAGRAM 222

WHITE TO MOVE

Do you see Black's threat? That's correct: On 2. Qxe2, Black has 2. ... Nh3 mate, with the Black Bishop on a8 taking away all of the light-colored escape squares. And if 2. Qxg5, then Black plays 2. ... Qf3, lining up the Bishop and Queen for a checkmate on either g2 or h1. Finally, if White tries to create a dark-colored escape square by 2. h4, then Black wins easily after 2. ... Nf3+. White, therefore, resigned rather than play on.

Pawn mates can occur in a variety of ways, including when promoting to a Queen, Rook, Bishop or Knight after reaching the other end of the board. A typical pawn mate motif involves a capture by a pawn which is also a mate because escape squares for the enemy King are guarded.

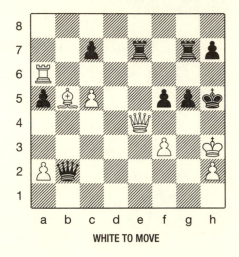

VIKTORS PUPOLS–CHRIS CORWIN
SEATTLE, 1968

DIAGRAM 223

WHITE TO MOVE

White ended the game by 1. Qg4+ fxg4+ 2. fxg4 mate. The entire sixth rank is surveyed by the Rook on a6. The lowly pawn is often mighty in chess, if not in real life, and chess wits have come up with more word games involving the pawn than any· other piece. Travel among chessplayers, and you will hear the true story of Pawnce de Leon, which will begin with the traditional storytelling phrase, "Once upawn a time."

Chess talk is all good, clean and excruciating fun.

CHESS MOVIE: CRAFT OR "WITCHCRAFT?"

Now it's time to follow the saga of a game decided through brilliant middlegame play. You are conducting the Black pieces with Robert J. ("Bobby") Fischer, whom many experts regard as the greatest player ever. In this game, which represents middlegame play at its most flawless, Bobby was accused by a few chess journalists of practicing "witchcraft," for he wins astonishingly quickly against a strong opponent who as White appears to make no mistakes. Analysts later discovered White's microscopic miscue, and so Bobby really won by practicing his stellar craft. GM Robert Byrne is the adversary, and the venue is the 1964 U.S. Championship. This classic game begins with 1. d4 Nf6 2. c4 g6 3. g3 c6 4. Bg2 d5 (see Diagram 224)—the Neo-Gruenfeld Defense.

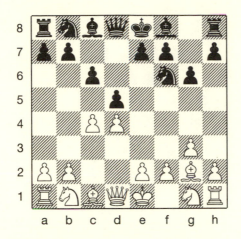

DIAGRAM 224

1. Play continues with 5. cxd5 cxd5 6. Nc3 Bg7 7. e3 0-0. Rather than physically placing their Bishops in the center, both sides try to control territory by using the diagonal-sweeping power of the clerics.

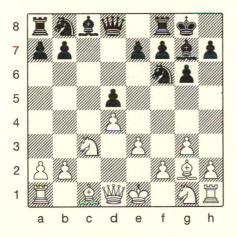

DIAGRAM 225

2. In top-flight chess the players typically complete their piece development before commencing tactical operations. The next moves are 8. Nge2 Nc6 9. 0-0 b6. Notice that these two grandmasters also move Knights and Bishops before Rooks and are fighting to control the center.

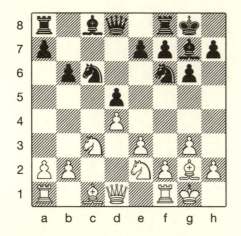

DIAGRAM 226

3. After 10. b3 Ba6 11. Ba3, the Black and White Queen Bishops are both striking toward the center even though located along the rim. Knights, however, cannot exercise power from afar; and an old chess adage is that a player who puts his Knights on the rim gets a trim. Well—usually.

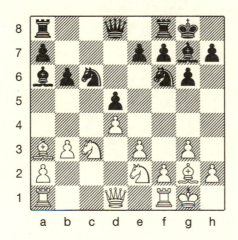

DIAGRAM 227

4. Black lashes out in the center with 11. ... Re8 12. Qd2 e5—a premature pawn eruption or strategy of the highest order? The answer is the latter, though while the game was being played, other grandmasters on the scene termed Fischer's bold pawn push a crude positional error.

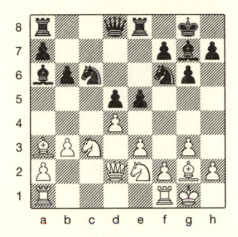

DIAGRAM 228

5. Here's why: 13. dxe5 Nxe5. Black's d-pawn is isolated, meaning that there is neither a c- nor e-pawn that can support it. White is already attacking the d-pawn with his Queen, c3-Knight and g2-Bishop. With proper preparation, he may win it.

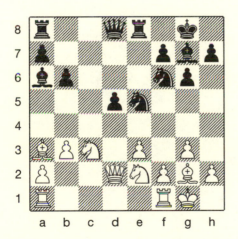

DIAGRAM 229

6. Employing this conventional wisdom, GM Byrne plays 14. Rfd1, piling up against the d-pawn. Fischer responds with 14. ... Nd3, creating an advanced center-file outpost. With hindsight, we now know that White needed to play 14. Rad1, when the position is approximately equal. Moving the Rook from f1 creates a fatal weakness on f2, which Black exploits.

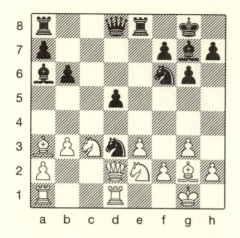

DIAGRAM 230

7. Can a grandmaster with the advantage of the White pieces and having made several good developing moves *really* lose a game because he removes protection from a single square? Against Fischer, yes! Byrne tries 15. Qc2, which uncovers the Rook at d1 directly against the Knight on d3, and Fischer plays 15. ... Nxf2!!.

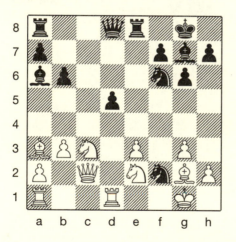

DIAGRAM 231

8. White has no realistic choice except to accept the proffered steed by 16. Kxf2, and Black continues the attack with 16. ... Ng4+. That the Knight sacrifice is correct will only be seen in Diagram 239. The most difficult combinations are those with the surprise point at the end.

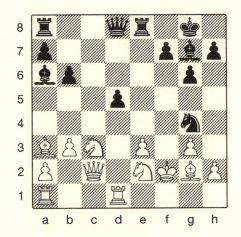

DIAGRAM 232

9. The White King retreats with 17. Kg1, and the Black Knight forks White's Queen and Rook by 17. ... Nxe3. The clash of opposing visions is quite dramatic: Byrne adopts a "Show me" attitude to what he judges to be a weak sacrifice, and Fischer responds, "Don't worry. I will."

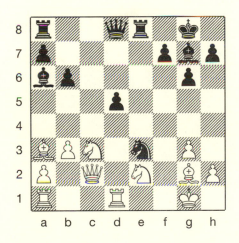

DIAGRAM 233

10. Byrne plays 18. Qd2, expecting Black to restore approximate material parity with 18. ... Nxd1, when grandmasters on the scene judged White to have a better position because of Black's weak d-pawn. But Fischer surprises with 18. ... Nxg2!, stripping cover from White's King.

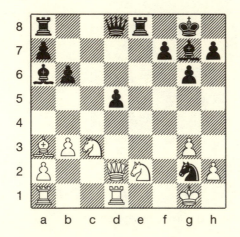

DIAGRAM 234

11. Black's target is the King, and he is willing to attack when a piece down. White takes the Knight with 19. Kxg2, and Fischer now voluntarily parts with the d-pawn that Byrne hoped to gain after a hard fight. The move is 19. ... d4, which opens the long a8-h1 diagonal on the King.

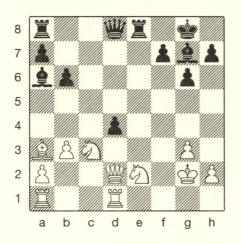

DIAGRAM 235

12. White bites at the bait with 20. Nxd4, and Black brings his Bishop to bear on the King by 20. ... Bb7+. Does Black have a strong enough attack for his piece? White cannot play 21. Kg1 because of 21. ... Bxd4+ 22. Qxd4 Re1+!! 23. Kf2 Qxd4 24. Rxd4 Rxa1, when Black wins. But what if ...

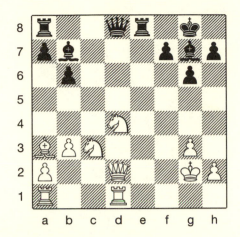

DIAGRAM 236

13. White plays 21. Kf1, which looks good. So good, in fact, that after Black responded with the quiet 21. ... Qd7, grandmasters on the scene predicted Fischer's speedy resignation. Instead came ... Byrne's resignation! What did the two players see that all of the spectators missed?

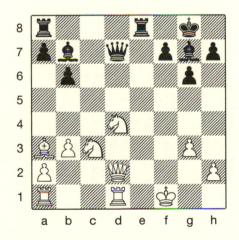

DIAGRAM 237

14. Everyone expected White to play 22. Qf2 and to meet 22. ... Qh3+, with 23. Kg1 as in the next diagram, when Bobby's attack appears to be dead. But the characteristic of Fischer's play that sets him apart from lesser mortals is an intuitive sense of when a position holds concealed possibilities.

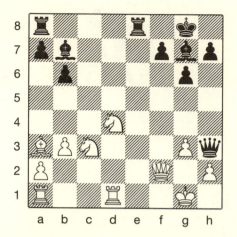

DIAGRAM 238

15. White's position looks absolutely secure because 23. ... Bxd4 fails against 24. Rxd4—though not 24. Qxd4 Qg2 mate. Black appears to have overshot the mark and to be down a piece without any further attack. Bobby's busted, right? Wrong! The sockdolager is 23. ... Re1+!!.

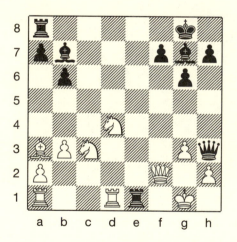

DIAGRAM 239

16. If 24. Qxe1, then 24. ... Qg2 mate; and if 24. Rxe1, then 24. ... Bxd4, threatening 25. ... Qg2, mate. Witchcraft? No, craft! But this master-piece demonstrates how the most minor misstep is punished at the highest level of chess.

8 Chessercizes for Taut Middlegames

MIDDLEGAME STRATEGY, TACTICAL devices and checkmates are the subjects of this quiz chapter. Can you distinguish between a splendid position bursting with mobile pieces and open lines and a constricted pretzel with pieces as mobile as football players beneath a pileup on the one-yard line? Are you able to employ tactical devices such as pins, double attacks, skewers and decoy sacrifices in over-the-board play?

And most importantly, after battering the opponent and building up a huge lead on points, can you deliver what the late, great American chess writer Al Horowitz used to call "the sockdolager," and what we in this more decorous volume usually call checkmate?

What follows is a chess test on the material in Chapter 7. In most instances, you are called upon to find a winning combination or plan. Try to use the analytical method given on page 161. First, look for threats against the well being of your position. Second, establish your goal (already provided in most of the questions). Finally, search for the tactical or strategic means to achieve the goal.

Just examine the position in each diagram, answer the questions and check your answers at the bottom of each page or on the following page. If your answer is wrong or, still worse, if you fail to understand why it is wrong, then review the relevant portion of Chapter 7.

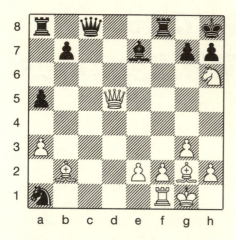

DIAGRAM 240

1. Demonstrate a smothered mate with White to move.

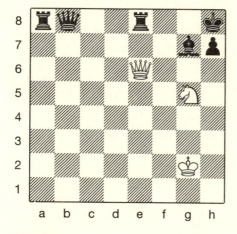

DIAGRAM 241

2. Demonstrate a smothered mate with White to move.

ANSWERS

1. The answer is a two-mover: 1. Qg8+ Rxg8 2. Nf7 mate. Although far behind in force, White wins because he has a local superiority in attacking force in the part of the board where it counts.

2. The classic four-move smothered mate sequence: 1. Nf7+ Kg8 2. Nh6+ Kh8 (the alternative is 2. ... Kf8 3. Qf7 mate) 3. Qg8+ Rxg8 4. Nf7 mate. Because Black's King is in double check from both the Queen and Knight on move 2, the second player must move the King. This fact prevents in every instance the capture of either the Queen or Knight and explains why the smothered mate sequence works.

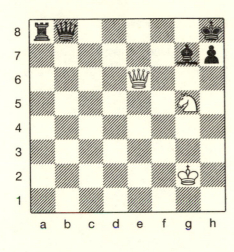

DIAGRAM 242

3. Can White force a smothered mate in this position?

DIAGRAM 243

4. White to move and mate in two moves.

ANSWERS

3. We hope and trust that you did not demonstrate a smothered mate sequence in this position because after 1. Nf7+ Kg8 2. Nh6+ Kh8 3. Qg8+ Qxg8 4. Nf7+, Black responds with 4. ... Qxf7 and wins easily. The most common reason for failing to deliver a smothered mate is that the mating square (f7 in this instance) is covered by an enemy piece that can capture the Knight. Therefore, White does best to take a draw by perpetual check after 3. Nf7+ Kg8 4. Nh6+ Kh8 (on 4. ... Kf8, White has 5. Qf7 mate) 5. Nf7+ and so on.

4. A variation on the smothering theme: 1. Qxh7+ Qxh7 2. Nf7 mate. The Queen sacrifice decoyed the Black Queen away from guarding the f7 square and lifted the pin on the Knight.

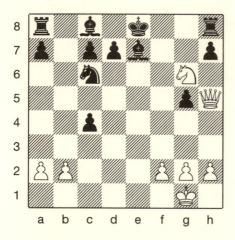

DIAGRAM 244

5. Demonstrate a smothered mate for White.

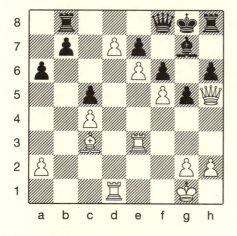

DIAGRAM 245

6. Use your positional judgment. With either side to move, who stands better?

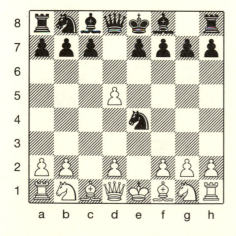

DIAGRAM 246

7. White to move and win material.

ANSWERS

5. The basic idea is identical to that in Chessercize 2. White smothers the Black King by 1. Ne5+ Kd8 (note: 1. ... Kf8 is again met by 2. Qf7 mate) 2. Nf7+ Ke8 3. Nd6+ (yes, the same double check device as before) 3. ... Kd8 4. Qe8+ Rxe8 5. Nf7 mate. This position is from Young–Dore (Boston, 1892).

6. White stands better—much better—no matter which side is on move. Give the diagram a purely visual inspection: Black has no piece beyond the second rank, and his four pieces on the Kingside are bunched together virtually immobile behind their pawns. The Queen Rook can move to precisely two squares (a8 and d8) without being captured, while the Queen has only the d8 square as a safe haven. Meanwhile, White has a pawn on d7 that may promote to a Queen at any moment and has highly mobile pieces covering 34 squares, compared to 9 squares for Black. In the actual game, Santasiere–Rose (Fort Lauderdale, 1966), White won quickly after 1. Ba5, threatening 2. d8=Q Rxd8 3. Rxd8, winning Black's Queen and mating shortly. After 1. ... Rd8 2. Rb3, Black resigned. White's unstoppable winning idea is simply 3. Rxb7 Kh7 (what else?) 4. Qg6+ Kg8 5. Bxd8 Qxd8 6. Rb8 Qxb8 7. d8=Q+ Qxd8 8. Rxd8 mate.

7. White wins the Black Knight with a double attack after 1. Qa4+ and 2. Qxe4. Queen checks by White on the d1-a4 and d1-h5 diagonals frequently pick up stray pieces; the same goes for Black on the d8-a5 and d8-h4 diagonals.

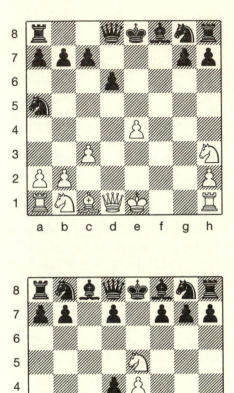

DIAGRAM 247

8. White to move and win material.

DIAGRAM 248

9. Black to move and win material.

ANSWERS

8. The correct check is 1. Qh5+ followed by 2. Qxa5. Black does not win back the piece by 2. ... Qh4+ because of 3. Nf2, shielding the King from check and rescuing the Knight. We hope and trust that you did not fall for 1. Qa4+, which is answered by 1. ... Nc6, when Black saves his Knight.

9. Just like White, Black can also spear a piece with a double attack by 1. ... Qa5+ and 2. ... Qxe5.

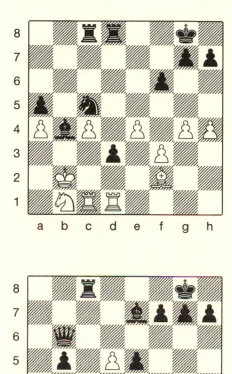

DIAGRAM 249

10. Black to move and win material with a Knight fork.

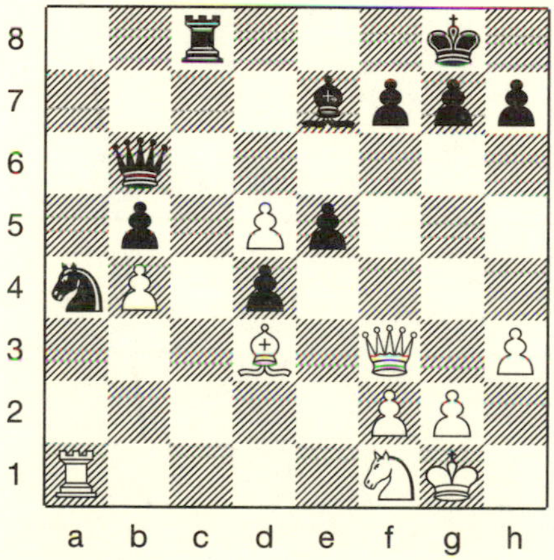

DIAGRAM 250

11. White to move and win decisive material.

ANSWERS

10. In game 47 of the 1984–85 world title match in Moscow, Garry Kasparov pulled off a neat Knight fork (a species of the double attack) against Anatoly Karpov by 1. ... d2 (attacking the Rook on c1 and vacating the d3 square for the Knight) 2. Rc2 Nd3+, White resigns. Black wins a Bishop in broad daylight.

11. Did you see that 1. Qf5 attacks both the Rook on c8 and threatens 2. Qxh7+ Kf8 3. Qh8 mate? Black must therefore surrender the Rook.

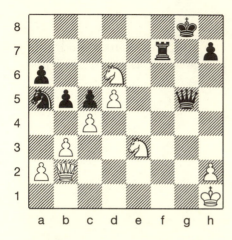

DIAGRAM 251

12. White to move and win immediately decisive material.

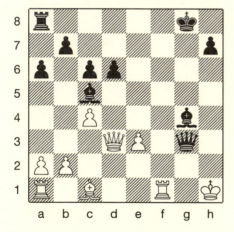

DIAGRAM 252

13. Use your positional judgment. With Black to move, who stands to win?

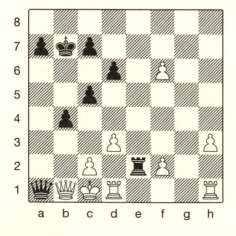

DIAGRAM 253

14. Black to move and mate in two moves.

ANSWERS

12. In world-class chess, grandmasters frequently string together a series of tactical devices in a single combination. From the 1966 world championship match held in Moscow, Tigran Petrosian as White can win a Rook against Boris Spassky after 1. Qh8+ Kxh8 2. Nxf7+ Kg7 3. Nxg5. (In the actual game, Black resigned after 1. Qh8+.) Notice how Qh8+ deflects the Black King from defense of the Rook and permits the double attack or fork by Nxf7+.

13. Black stands much better and is close to winning outright. In terms of force, White is up a Rook for a Bishop (2 points), but Black has an extra pawn. So, White's edge here is a minimal 1 point. But the important factor is that White's Queenside pieces are useless, while Black enjoys a large local superiority in force against the vulnerable enemy King. White's single useful piece is the King Rook, which dominates the f-file. Black decides to challenge this control by bringing into action his last undeveloped piece. Rooks love open files, and the move is 1. ... Rf8, threatening 2. ... Rxf1+ 3. Qxf1 Bf3+. Black either wins the Queen or mates. Defense by 2. Rxf8+ Kxf8 3. Qf1+ is met by 3. ... Bf3+. Actual play continued 2. Bd2 Bf3+ 3. Rxf3 Qxf3+ 4. Kg1 (if 4. Kh2, Black finishes the game by 4. ... Qf2+ 5. Kh1 Qh4+ 6. Kg1 Rf2 and 7. ... Qh2 mate) 4. ... Rf4, White resigns. White cannot play 5. exf4 because of the Bishop pin on the King. Black will continue with 5. ... Rg4+, and White is in a mating net.

14. Think field marshals and shoulder boards, for 1. ... Rxc2+ 2. Kxc2 Qc3 is an epaulette mate. The escape of the White King is prevented by its own pieces.

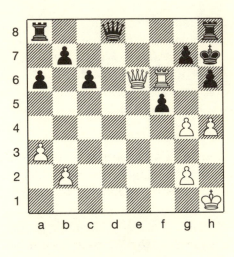

DIAGRAM 254

15. White to move and mate in two moves.

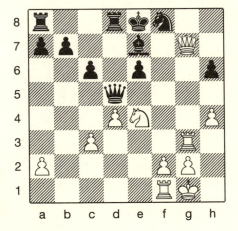

DIAGRAM 255

16. White to move and mate in three moves.

ANSWERS

15. A golden oldie. The scene is Vienna 1861, and Wilhelm Steinitz, official world champion from 1886 to 1894, scores an epaulette by 1. Rxh6+ gxh6 2. Qf7 mate. Once again, the retreat squares of h6 and h8, which the mating piece does not control, are blocked by Black's own men.

16. In Korchnoi–Petersen (Kiev, 1964), White produced an epaulette by 1. Qxe7+ Kxe7 2. Rg7+ Ke8 3. Nf6 mate. Viktor Korchnoi (born in 1931), the player with the White pieces, is regarded by many as the strongest player never to win the world championship. Twice—in matches sanctioned by the International Chess Federation in 1974 and 1978—Korchnoi missed becoming world champion by only a single point.

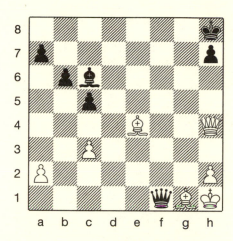

DIAGRAM 256

17. Black to move and mate in two moves.

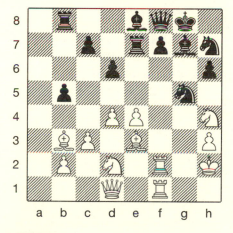

DIAGRAM 257

18. Use your positional judgment. With either side to move, who stands better?

ANSWERS

17. Back in 1899, against an amateur player, America's Harry Nelson Pillsbury (1872–1906) wins brilliantly by 1. ... Qf3+ 2. Bxf3 Bxf3 mate—another epaulette. Pillsbury was regarded as a likely world champion until his early death.

18. White stands better. The position is from Tarrasch–Burn (Ostend, 1907). White enjoys open lines for his pieces, with his Queen able to roam on either side of the board and with the Rooks powerfully doubled on the f-file. Meanwhile, Black's Queen has no moves, and he has only one piece developed beyond his second rank. In a sentence, Black has little space and less piece mobility. White played 1. Ng6, attacking the smothered Queen, and Black resigned. Did you notice that 1. ... fxg6 is impossible because of the Bishop pin along the a2-g8 diagonal?

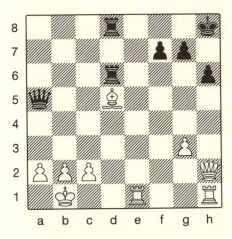

DIAGRAM 258

19. White now plays 1. Bb3. Who ought to win?

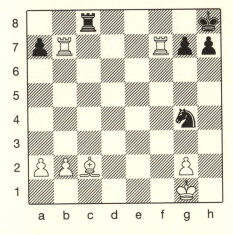

DIAGRAM 259

20. White plays the double attack 1. Bf5. Can Black save material?

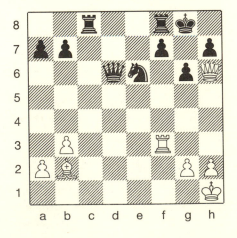

DIAGRAM 260

21. White to move and mate in three moves.

ANSWERS

19. If you answered White, then check the steps of the analytical method given on page 161. The first player neglected to examine the opponent's threats before removing his Bishop from attack by playing 1. Bb3. Black now forces a back-rank mate with 1. ... Qxe1+ 2. Rxe1 Rd1+ 3. Rxd1 Rxd1 mate. Simply 1. c4, protecting the Bishop with a pawn, maintains White's large material advantage. With reasonable play, White wins easily.

20. In a technical sense, yes. The move, 1. ... Rc4, removes the Rook from attack and protects the Knight. Unfortunately, it also permits 2. Rf8 mate. Correct is the exceedingly simple 1. ... Rc1 mate. In his haste to win still more material, White either forgot that the Black Knight guarded both f2 and h2 or failed to notice that the Bishop on f5 cut off the retreat of the Rook back to f1, guarding against the mate. By using the analytical method before moving, White would have checked possible Black threats and might have played the easily winning 1. Rbc7, squelching the attack on the Bishop.

21. Another back-rank mate that is set up by a Queen sacrifice! Here is the finish: 1. Qxh7+ Kxh7 2. Rh3+ Kg8 3. Rh8 mate. The cooperation of Bishop with Rook to mate a King on the back rank is a very common pattern.

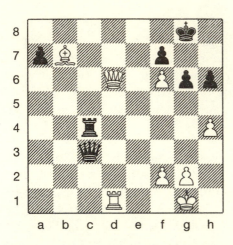

DIAGRAM 261

22. White to move and mate in two moves.

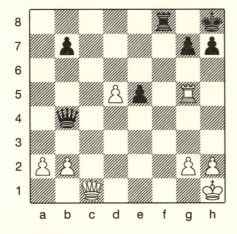

DIAGRAM 262

23. Black to move and win immediately decisive material.

ANSWERS

22. Rook and pawns also cooperate to produce back-rank mates as in 1. Qf8+ Kxf8 2. Rd8 mate. On 1. ... Kh7, White plays 2. Qg7 mate. The creator of this combination is Tatiana Zatulovskaya, one of the world's top women players. And don't forget the idea of sacrificing a Queen to decoy the King to a square (in this instance, f8) where it can be mated.

23. In Lowtzky–Tartakower (Jurata, 1937), Black came up with the inspired 1. ... Qd2!, a double attack on the Queen and Rook and a move also threatening the very simple 2. ... Qxc1 mate. White cannot play 2. Qxd2 because of the back-ranking 2. ... Rf1 mate, and he must therefore move his Queen and lose the Rook.

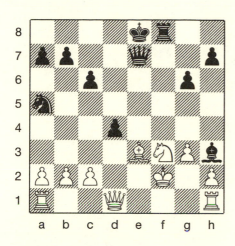

DIAGRAM 263

24. Black to move and win.

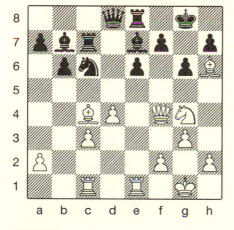

DIAGRAM 264

25. White to move and mate in two moves.

ANSWERS

24. Paul Morphy (1837–84), the "pride and sorrow" of nineteenth-century American chess, crisscrossed Judge A.B. Meek with 1. ... Qxe3 mate. Morphy was the greatest player of the nineteenth century, destroying with consummate ease the strongest European masters in the space of a few months in 1858 and 1859. At which point, he never played serious competitive chess again. No player since Morphy has so completely dominated his contemporaries.

25. White found the unexpected 1. Qxf7+, and Black resigned rather than face 1. ... Kxf7 2. Bxe6 mate or 1. ... Kh8 2. Qg7 mate.

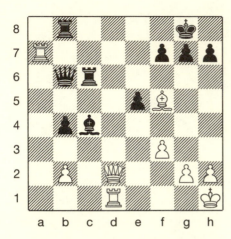

DIAGRAM 265

26. White to move and win immediately decisive material.

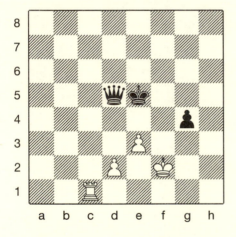

DIAGRAM 266

27. White to move and draw.

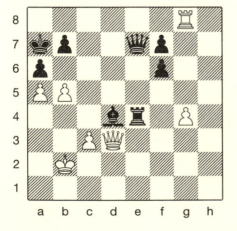

DIAGRAM 267

28. White to move and force mate.

ANSWERS

26. We're betting that you missed this one. In Mileika–Voitkevich (Riga, 1963), White found the utterly stunning knock-out blow, 1. Rb7!!!, a double attack on the Rook and Queen that also threatens 2. Rxb8+ Qxb8 3. Qd8+ Qxd8 4. Rxd8 mate. Further, Black cannot capture the Rook because of Qd8+ in reply, leading again to a back-rank mate. The point behind 1. Rb7!!! is to deflect one of Black's two pieces away from guarding the d8 square. If Black tries to avoid mate with, say, 1. ... Rbc8, then the simple 2. Rxb6 wins easily..

27. Black is up a Queen for a Rook and pawn and menaces 1. ... Qf3+, followed by pushing in the g-pawn for a second Queen. But the decoy sacrifice of 1. Rc5 pins the Queen on the King and threatens to capture the lady. Black has nothing better than 1. ... Qxc5, when there is a skin-and-bones draw after 2. d4+ (a pawn fork or double attack) 2. ... Qxd4 3. exd4+ Kxd4 4. Kg3 and 5. Kxg4. Notice that this combination contained tactical devices such as a decoy sacrifice, a pin and a double attack.

28. In Spassky–Petrosian (Moscow, 1967), there is a pawn mate after 1. Qxd4+ Rxd4 2. b6 mate. Another conclusion could be 1. ... b6 2. Qxb6 mate. The key factor in this mating pattern is the Rook on the eighth ranking guarding all of Black's escape squares.

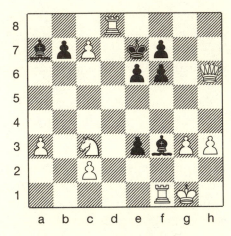

DIAGRAM 268

29. White threatens 2. Qf8 mate. Can Black now force a checkmate with his pawn on e3?

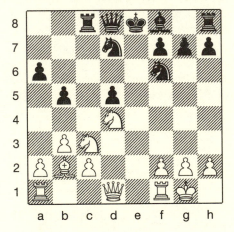

DIAGRAM 269

30. Use your positional judgment. With White to move, who stands better?

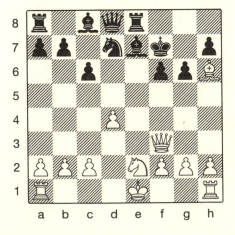

DIAGRAM 270

31. Can White win this position?

ANSWERS

29. Yes, but how? As Black in a game played at Monterey, California, in 1971, Russo-American master Alex Suhobeck winds up the battle with 1. ... e2+ 2. Kh2 exf1=N mate. If White instead plays 2. Rf2, then 2. ... e1=Q+ 3. Kh2 (the only legal move) 3. ... Qh1 mate or 3. ... Qxf2 mate. Promoting to a Knight, Rook or Bishop rather than to a Queen is called *underpromotion*.

30. Remember your lessons from the chapters on the opening and middlegame. Do Kings belong in the center of the board? Do Rooks lust for wide open files? No, yes. White clearly stands better, and the game continues 1. Re1+ (grabbing a center file) 1. ... Be7 (if 1. ... Ne4, White wins the Knight by 2. f3, hitting the pinned piece) 2. Nf5 (threatening to win at least a piece by 3. Rxe7+) 2. ... Ng8 (undeveloping his Knight but defending the Bishop) 3. Nxd5, when White adds a third attack on the pinned Bishop on e7. Do you see how the check by the Rook along the open central file sets up a pin, which leads to winning at least a piece? A pin by Rooks or Queen on a central file is a very strong strategic idea that often leads to tactical fireworks as the pressure builds. And do not forget: Doubling Rooks or a Queen and Rook along a file can be still stronger in many positions.

31. Did you see the win (1. Qb3 mate!)? This mate is a variation on the two-Bishop crisscross mate given in Chapter 7. The defining characteristic here is the scissor-like control of the light and dark squares.

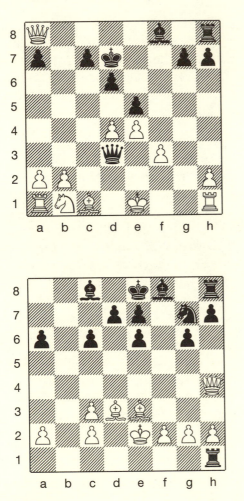

DIAGRAM 271

32. Black to move and win.

DIAGRAM 272

33. After 1. Qxh7 Rxh7, how does White checkmate in two moves?

ANSWERS

32. A crisscross from afar is the theme in Rodzinsky–Alekhine (Moscow, 1913). The move is 1. ... Be7, and the game ended quickly after 2. Qxh8 Bh4 mate. The Queen not only blocks the f1 escape square, it also holds the d-file. A move to avoid mate such as 2. h4 is answered very simply by 2. ... Rxa8, picking up White's Queen.

33. The answer is a very rare, perhaps unique two-Bishop mate by 2. Bxg6+ Kd8 3. Bb6 mate. It was literally thought up by Latvian-American master Viktors Pupols during a ... dream!

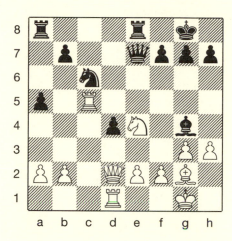

DIAGRAM 273

34. Pin punishes sin (1. h3?).
Black to move and win
material.

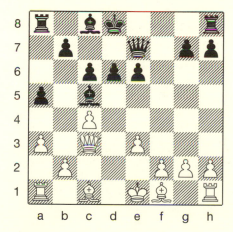

DIAGRAM 274

35. Black to move and win
material.

ANSWERS

34. Garry Kasparov has been world chess kingpin since 1985, and one
reason is his incredible alertness to tactical possibilities. In Nikolic–
Kasparov (Niksic, 1983), White has just played 1. h3?, which is refuted
by 1. ... Bxe2, snagging a pawn. White cannot play 2. Qxe2 because of
2. ... Qxc5 3. Nxc5 Rxe2, winning a Rook and pawn for a Bishop.

35. In Turner–Parr (Bellevue, 1972), Black noticed a trick in a seemingly
innocuous position: 1. ... Bb4 (a surprise pin) 2. axb4 (apparently
picking off the Bishop in broad daylight) 2. ... axb4 (suddenly, an
attack on the Queen at c3 and a discovered attack on the Rook at a1)
3. Qxb4 Rxa1 (winning a Rook for a Bishop). The lesson: Look twice
to see if an apparently unlikely move, 1. ... Bb4, is actually possible.

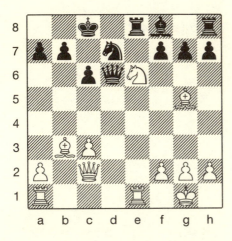

DIAGRAM 275

36. Use your positional judgment. With Black to move, who stands better?

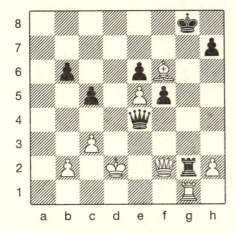

DIAGRAM 276

37. White pins the Rook at g2 on the Black King, and Black pins the Queen at f2 on the White King. With Black to move, can he win?

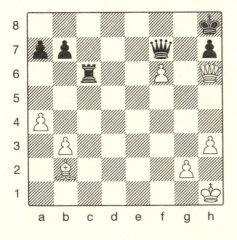

DIAGRAM 277

38. White to move, pin and win by mate.

ANSWERS

36. White stands better, even though Black is up a pawn after the forced capture of the Knight by 1. ... fxe6. White's advantage consists of a huge lead in time (Black's Kingside pieces on f8 and h8 are blocked in and doing nothing), and a major advantage in mobility (not only are the pieces on f8 and h8 immobile, so in effect is Black's Rook on e8, which is limited to defending the e6-pawn, while White's castle on e1 is sweeping down the file on the pawn in conjunction with the Bishop on b3). In addition, White's Bishop on g5 is eyeing such relevant central-file squares as e7 and d8 in the event that Black should try to play the Rook to either square. Keeping in mind our theme that Rooks lust for open files and no more heartily than for central files, White can get his last inactive piece into the fray by 2. Rad1, attacking the Queen and forcing it to move. Black's problem is that he has no satisfactory move. On 2. ... Qc7, the capture 3. Bxe6 pins the Knight, and the defense 3. ... Bd6 is answered by 4. Qd2, which skewers the Knight on d7. Black tries 2. ... Qc5, attacking the Bishop on g5, but White relentlessly centralizes by doubling Queen and Rook on the d-file with 3. Qd2, intending 4. Qxd7+ with mate coming up. Black has no defense. On 3. ... Nb6, the finish might be 4. Bxe6+ Rxe6 5. Qd8 mate. The control of central files by the Queen and Rooks and the additional ploy of doubling these pieces on these files is a very powerful strategic idea that usually augurs tactical success.

37. In Franklin–Golombek (British Championship, 1962), Black cut the Gordian Pin with 1. ... Qf4+, a double attack on the King and the still-pinned White Queen, which cannot capture its counterpart. Black wins easily. Talk about pins, counter-pins and needles!

38. Did you see the winning move? Watch: 1. Qf8+ Qxf8 2. f7+ Rf6 (a move delaying the inevitable) 3. Bxf6+ Qg7 4. f8=Q mate. The absolute pin by the Bishop on the Queen cannot be broken, and the pawn promotion is, therefore, a checkmate.

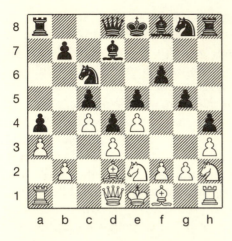

DIAGRAM 278

39. Use your positional judgment. With either side to move, who stands better?

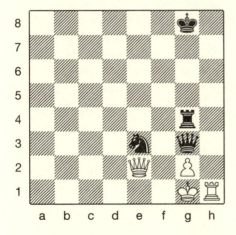

DIAGRAM 279

40. Black to move and mate in two moves.

DIAGRAM 280

41. Black to move and mate in two moves. Does 1. ... Nh3 also win, although more slowly?

ANSWERS

39. From Taubenhaus–Tarrasch (Hamburg, 1885). Although there is no immediate win in sight, Black enjoys a distinct advantage in space and piece mobility. While Black can effortlessly develop his Kingside forces and maneuver his Queenside pieces, White's pieces lack scope because potential development squares are controlled by Black's pawns. The Bishop on d2 can only retreat to c1. The Knight on e2 can go only to c1 or g1. And the White Queen is also confined. As for White's Bishop at f1 and his Rook at h1, they are completely hemmed in. In the further course of the game, White tried to break out of the bind but was trampled when Black's more mobile forces rushed into the breach. The typical course of a game in which one side is short of space features a failed attempt to escape encirclement, followed by defeat.

40. A basic pattern of the Arabian Knight mate: 1. ... Qxg2+ 2. Qxg2 Rxg2 mate. Notice how the Knight guards the f1 escape square. Or maybe you spotted the attractive alternative pointed out by our colleague, Grandmaster and five-time U.S. Champion Larry Evans: 1. ... Qe1+ 2. Qxe1 Rxg2 mate!

41. A typical Arabian Knight ambush. After 1. ... Nf3, the White King is corralled on h1 because the Rook controls the second rank and the Knight hits g1, thereby forcing 2. h4 (or 2. h3), when 2. ... Rh2 is mate. We hope and trust that you did not answer yes to 1. ... Nh3 being a slower win because it is no win at all. It is a draw by stalemate!

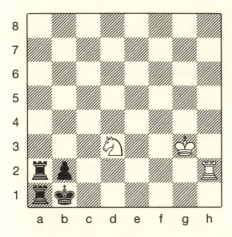

DIAGRAM 281

42. With Black to move, who wins? With White to move, who wins?

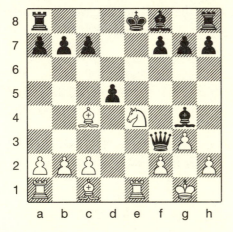

DIAGRAM 282

43. White to move and mate in two moves.

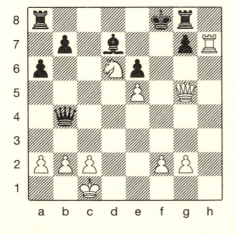

DIAGRAM 283

44. White to move and mate in two moves.

ANSWERS

42. Vladimir Korolkov (1907–1987), a great Russian composer of chess problems and puzzles, invented this position *circa* 1950. White wins no matter who is on move. If Black moves his Rook on a2 (his only legal play!), then White mates with Rxb2. If White moves, he loses a tempo—which is to say, deliberately makes a time-wasting move with, say, Rg2, Rf2 or Kf3, Kh3—thereby forcing Black to move his a2-Rook, when White again mates with Rxb2. The ploy of losing a tempo occurs quite often in endgames where the weaker party enjoys an otherwise tenable position except for being obliged to make a move.

43. Most Arabian mates occur in corners, though not this one: 1. Nf6+ Kd8 2. Re8 mate. Notice that the Knight once again commands a key escape square—this time d7. As for Black, since he was in double check, he was forced to move his King to its only available square.

44. In Alekhine–Asgierssen (Reykjavik, 1931), White conjured up a romantic Arabian Knight with 1. Qf6+ gxf6 2. Rf7 mate. The Queen sacrifice was necessary to open the seventh rank for White's mating Rook.

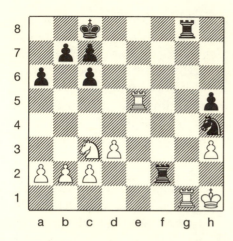

DIAGRAM 284

45. Black to move and mate in three moves.

DIAGRAM 285

46. White to move and force mate. Hint: Rooks hunger for open files.

ANSWERS

45. This three-mover from Tartakower–Schlechter (Vienna, 1908) is a toughie. Did you see 1. ... Rh2+!! 2. Kxh2 Nf3+ 3. Kh1 Rxg1 mate, an Arabian mate preceded by a fork or double attack with 2. ... Nf3+?

46. White is behind a Queen, Rook and Knight, but there is always hope when a completely open file—in this instance, the g-file—leads to the enemy King. Rooks lust for open files, and White mates by 1. Nh6+ (don't forget the Bishop at b2 raking the dark squares next to Black's King) 1. ... Nxh6 2. Rg1+ Qg3 3. Rxg3+ Ng4 4. Rxg4+ Bg5 5. Rxg5 mate.

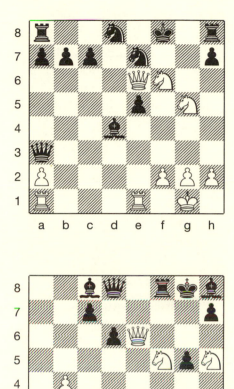

DIAGRAM 286

47. White to move and mate in two moves.

DIAGRAM 287

48. After 1. ... Bxe6, what is White's best move?

ANSWERS

47. In Clemens–Eisenschmidt (Dorpat, 1862), White pulled off a much admired two-Knight mate by 1. Qf7+ Nxf7 2. Ne6 mate. The two Knights command all of the escape squares, but notice that the real trick was to force Black's Knight to f7 via the Queen sacrifice.

48. After 1. ... Bxe6, there is not much horsing around after 2. Nh6 mate. This two-Knight mate could also be classified as an epaulette mate because the King is prevented from escaping by his own pieces on two adjacent squares.

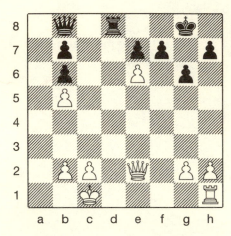

DIAGRAM 288

49. Use your positional judgment. With Black to move,
does he stand better? Hint:
Think about the "heart-
break" mate.

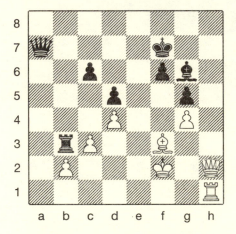

DIAGRAM 289

50. White to move and win
material. Hint: Think about
the "shish-kebab" tactical
device.

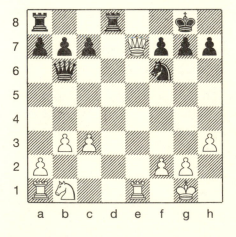

DIAGRAM 290

51. Black to move and win
immediately decisive
material.

ANSWERS

49. In this position from Quiñones–Smyslov (Amsterdam, 1964), the factor of space is approximately even. Both sides have plenty of roaming room for their pieces, and no one is dominating the center. As for material, it is dead even. However, Black has an advantage in both time (his Rook is developed and White's is not) and King safety. Both of these advantages could be fleeting unless Black can find a winning plan before White catches up in development next move. Our hint reads, think "heartbreak" mate. Black wins by taking our oft-repeated advice to grab open files. He plays 1. ... Qa7, threatening a back-rank mate with 2. ... Qa1, since the King cannot escape to d2 thanks to the Black Rook bearing down on the central d-file. White tried 2. exf7+ and resigned after 2. ... Kf8. If 3. Kb1, then Black has 3. ... Ra8 4. c3 Qa1+ 5. Kc2 Qxh1, finishing up a full Rook. Vassily Smyslov, the winner of this game, was world champion from 1957 to 1958 and was renowned for his endgame play.

50. Try to solve this position by employing the analytical method on page 161. Establish a goal and seek the tactical device that will help you to reach that goal. Here the attainable goal is a skewer or the so-called "shish-kebab" tactic: 1. Qh7+ Bxh7 2. Rxh7+ Ke6 3. Rxa7, winning a Bishop.

51. Another skewer. Black picks up decisive material by 1. ... Re8, hitting the Rook on e1 if the Queen moves. Notice that Black calculated that he had adequate protection for his e8-Rook and would not suffer a back-rank mate after 2. Qxe8+ Rxe8 3. Rxe8+ Nxe8.

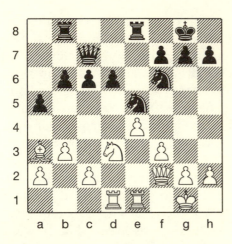

DIAGRAM 291

52. White to move and win material.

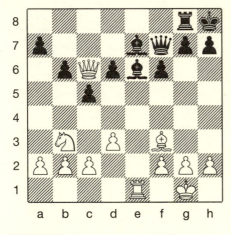

DIAGRAM 292

53. After 1. Qe4 Bd7, can White take the Bishop on e7?

ANSWERS

52. The skewer is hidden until White opens his d-file for the Rook with 1. Nxe5 dxe5, when he suddenly has both Rook and Bishop striking the d6 square. He continues 2. Bd6, skewering the Rook on b8 after 2. ... Qb7 3. Bxb8.

53. No! Remember back-rank mates. After 1. Qe4 Bd7 2. Qxe7 Re8, White cannot play 3. Qxf7 because of 3. ... Rxe1 mate. His best chance is to give up the Queen by 3. Qxe8+, though Black still has an edge in force (a Queen for Rook and Knight) and should win over the long haul.

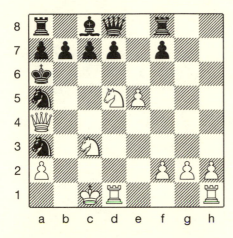

DIAGRAM 293

54. White to move and mate in three moves. Hint: White does a lot of horsing around.

DIAGRAM 294

55. After 1. ... Ng3, did White do the smart thing by resigning the game?

ANSWERS

54. In I. Zaitsev–Skotorenko (Soviet Union, 1970), White pulled off a marvelously hidden two-Knighter: 1. Qb5+ Nxb5 2. Nb4+ Kb6 3. Na4 mate. Once again, a Queen sacrifice forced Black to block a potential escape square (b5), setting up the mate.

55. Yes, White was fully justified in resigning after 1. ... Ng3. His Queen is attacked twice by the Knight and Queen, and if 2. Qxg6, then 2. ... Nde2 mate. This beautiful coup occurred in Marache–Morphy (New York, 1857).

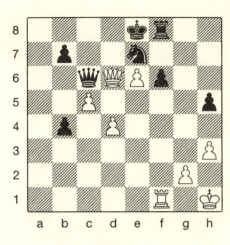

DIAGRAM 295

56. Use your positional judgment. With White to move, does he stand better?

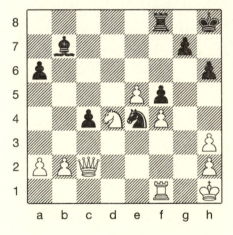

DIAGRAM 296

57. Black to move and mate in two moves.

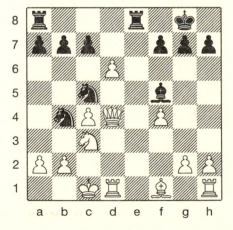

DIAGRAM 297

58. Black to move and mate in two moves.

ANSWERS

56. Taken from Morphy–Thompson (New York, 1860), this position requires careful evaluation. Take some time to consider the possibilities. Black is up a Knight for a pawn, but White has an obvious edge in King safety and in space with his advancing herd of center pawns and active Rook compared to Black's bunched up Knight and Rook, which are fulfilling strictly defensive tasks. The question is whether White's edge in space and time compensates for Black's advantage in force. In this instance, it does. Morphy took our advice about using Rooks to grab open files and played 1. Ra1, intending 2. Ra8+ Nc8 3. e7, threatening 4. exf8=Q mate, and if 3. ... Qxd6, then 4. cxd6. White is attacking both the Knight and the Rook, and Black has no way to avoid decisive material loss.

57. The Bishop and Knight mating pattern is both piquant and often surprising because the losing side seems to have plenty of escape squares, but the surprising cooperation between Bishop and Knight can cover them all. In Torres–Alekhine (Seville, 1922), we have a typical Bishop and Knight mate after 1. ... Nf2+ 2. Kg1 Nxh3. Notice that f2 is covered by the Knight and g2 by the Bishop.

58. After 1. ... Nxa2+, there are two beautiful mates after either 2. Nxa2 Nb3 mate or 2. Kd2 Nb3. Notice that in the first mate, the Knight scopes out d2 while the Bishop strikes b1 and c2.

DIAGRAM 298

59. Why did Black resign in this position, when it was his turn to move?

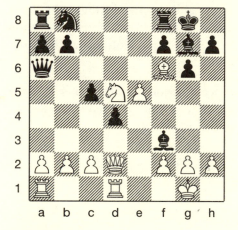

DIAGRAM 299

60. White to move and force mate.

ANSWERS

59. From Spassky–Marszalek (Leningrad, 1960). White has just played 1. Qg5-h6 with the obvious threat of 2. Qxg7 mate. And if 1. ... gxh6, then White has 2. Nxh6 mate, another Bishop and Knighter. As for 1. ... Bf6, White plays 2. Bxf6, with mate coming up.

60. In Bednarski–Nouissere (Siegen, 1970), White's bolt from the blue was 1. Qh6, threatening 2. Qxg7 mate. If 1. ... Bxh6, then 2. Ne7 mate. The sacrifice 1. Qh6 decoys the g7-Bishop off the long diagonal, permitting the Bishop and Knight mate.

⑨ *Endgame Strategy and Checkmates*

FORGIVE US FOR DEFINING the ending as "the phase of the game—the final phase—that follows the opening and middlegame." Such a definition, though accurate and obligatory in chess writing, says little about the specific features of endgames.

If the opening is about building a position and the middlegame about formulating plans to achieve goals, then the ending involves exploiting whatever possibilities were created by the opening and middlegame. Planning remains exceedingly important, and the imperatives of the analytical method still apply.

ENDGAME: IDENTIFYING CHARACTERISTICS

Here is a happy fact if you are winning in the endgame and a loathsome one if you are losing: Whatever advantage that may exist for one side in the ending is more likely to be permanent or decisive than in the earlier phases. After all, the struggle is necessarily nearer its conclusion. The stronger side has fewer opportunities to err, and the weaker side has fewer chances to recoup past losses.

Also, material advantages in the ending generally loom larger than in the preceding phases. Losing two pawns in the opening is fatal about 70 percent of the time among amateurs, but being down two pawns in the endgame is fatal 95 percent of the time among these same amateurs. For example, Black is a cooked goose in the following position, which is also a good example of another key characteristic of endings—that is, reduced material or, quite simply, fewer pieces and often fewer pawns:

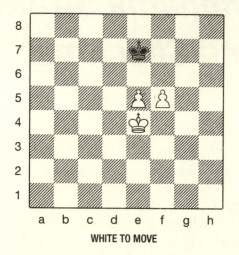

DIAGRAM 300

WHITE TO MOVE

White's win is exceedingly simple, no matter who is on move. Here is a typical way to win this position, though there are dozens of continuations that win just as easily.

1.	Kd5	Kd7
2.	e6+	Ke7
3.	Ke5	Ke8
4.	Kd6	

White can also win with 4. f6. The point is that there are many winning moves.

4.	...	Kd8

Just as White has many ways to win, Black has many ways to lose. On 4. ... Kf8, White plays 5. Kd7, taking control of the Queening square at e8 and then pushing the e-pawn forward to make a Queen.

5.	e7+	Ke8

Yes, White can also play 5. f6, forcing 5. ... Ke8 to stop the f-pawn from going straight in. White then wins by 6. f7+ Kf8 7. Kd7, taking control once again of e8.

6.	f6	

Here is the only sensitive moment in winning this ending. Just remember not to permit a stalemate by 6. Ke6—the possibility of which is the only reason why Black would wish to keep playing.

6.	...	Kf7

7.	Kd7	Kxf6

8.   e8=Q, and White wins

With King and Queen against King, White can mate easily, as will be demonstrated later in this chapter.

In terms of the role of the various pieces, the biggest difference between the endgame and the middlegame or opening is the role of the King. If in the opening one's duty is to get the King castled into a corner and out of harm's way and if in the middlegame the requirement is to keep the King safe and usually away from the center of the board, then in the endgame a crucial requirement is to centralize the King so as to make it a fighting piece.

The reason for the differing King roles between the middlegame and endgame is obvious, and we gave explanatory examples on page 148 and page 149 of Chapter 7. A centralized King during the middlegame is subject to attack from an array of pieces, usually including a Queen, Rooks and one or more minor pieces. In a typical pared-down ending involving only a few pieces on each side, the King is in far less danger; the player who centralizes his King for fighting purposes will in effect be a piece ahead against an opponent who keeps his King in its castled position.

In most endings, pawns grow slightly in relative importance against pieces. The main reason for a shift in fighting value is that impediments to Queening grow less as pieces gets exchanged and as the pawns advance up the board. Pawn promotions are common in the endgame; they are exceedingly rare in openings and unusual in middlegames. In the endgame below, White enjoys an advantage in force (a Knight versus two pawns), and he also has his King much closer to the action than does Black. Yet the second player wins very simply.

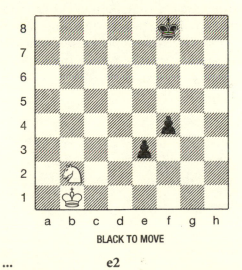

DIAGRAM 301

BLACK TO MOVE

1.	...	e2

Black threatens to make a Queen with 2. ... e1=Q+, and White's reply is, therefore, forced.

2.   Nd3   f3

Intending 3. ... f2 4. Nxf2 e1=Q+. Very simple.

3.   Kc2

The Knight has no useful move, and White's only chance is to bring his King closer. The other move, 3. Kc1, also loses.

3.   ...   f2

4.   Nxf2   e1=Q and wins

White's alternative of 4. Kd2 is obviously met by 4. ... f1=Q. If Black's pawns were farther up the board on, say, e6 and f5, there would be no forced win. White could block the advance of the pawns fairly easily with his King and Knight. But in the actual endgame position with Black's pawns well advanced and close to Queening, White's King and Knight are unable to coordinate quickly enough to mount a defense.

The pawns became mighty.

In our chapters on the opening and middlegame, we preached insistently about the value of time or making every move count. In many of the examples we gave, it was obvious that if one side skipped moves and permitted the other side (against the rules, of course) a series of free moves, then he would commit suicide. The side having free moves would line up his pieces advantageously, capture inconvenient enemy pieces, and place the opposing King in checkmate.

The endgame can be far different. In most instances, the right (and obligation) to move is still an advantage, but there can be times when any move that you have available makes your position worse. Chess people have adopted the German word *zugzwang* (meaning "compulsion to move") to describe such situations. When a player is faced with a position where all available moves are undesirable, we say the player is "in *zugzwang*," and the position itself is "a *zugzwang*."

DIAGRAM 302

In the above position, neither player wishes to be the first to move, and thus both are in *zugzwang*. If White moves first, he cannot win the game because his options are 1. Kd6 stalemate or moving the King away from the pawn, when Black draws after capturing it. If Black moves first, he loses the game after 1. ... Kc7 (the only legal move) 2. Ke7. White now has control of the Queening square d8 and will make a Queen next move.

Frequently, the stronger side can force the weaker side into *zugzwang* by playing a **waiting move**, which is a move that alters nothing of consequence in the position while shifting the turn to the opponent.

DIAGRAM 303

BLACK TO MOVE

White could draw this position if he never had to move because, given the array of the White King and Bishop, you can't place the Black King and Rook anywhere to create a checkmate. Yet, if White moves first, he gets mated after 1. Kh1 (the only legal move) 1. ... Rxf1. So, when faced with having to move in this position, Black must find a way to "return" the move to White without altering the dynamics of the position. Black plays

one of four waiting moves—1. ... Rb1, 1. ... Rc1, 1. ... Rd1 or 1. ... Re1—
which then forces White to move his King into the corner, where it gets
mated.

The purpose of a waiting move is, in effect, to lose a move and to force
the other side to make a self-destructive move.

BASIC ENDGAME STRATEGY

Endgame strategy can be boiled down to making plans that enable the
stronger side to

- Create a passed pawn.

- Transform a passed pawn into a Queen.

- Exploit a material advantage that is sufficient to force checkmate.

That's all.

Of course, there is a lot involved in devising plans that can accomplish
these goals.

Most endgames come down to creating a passed pawn and then con-
verting it into a Queen. Indeed, the core of endgame strategy is devising
plans for creating a passed pawn and advancing it to promotion.

Making a passed pawn requires eliminating the enemy pawn directly
in front of the planned passer and the two adjacent enemy pawns. You
may sacrifice material to eliminate these pawns or capture them during
the game. You can also lure enemy pawns out of the way through mutual
pawn exchanges or by exchanges of pieces and pawns. Take, for example,
the following position, which demands a plan both for creating a passed
pawn and for ushering it forward to promotion:

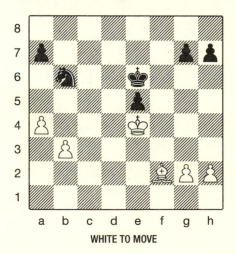

DIAGRAM 304

WHITE TO MOVE

Here is how the White player might analyze the situation: "Well, none of my men is exposed to capture, and my King is safe. But how do I win when material is even, and my opponent has the only passed pawn, although its advance is blocked by my King? Wait, I can also create a passed pawn by playing 1. Bxb6 axb6 2. b4, when the threat is a4-a5. Black must now sashay his King over to the a-file to stop the upcoming passer. So, he tries 2. ... Kd6, and play continues 3. a5 bxa5 4. bxa5 Kc6. Black has no choice: He must stop my a-pawn, which allows me to capture his e-pawn with 5. Kxe5—and all the rest of his pawns after 5. ... Kb5 6. Ke6 Kxa5 7. Kf7 g5 ('You can run, but you can't hide!') 8. Kg7 h5 9. Kg6. I now win one of the pawns and the second a bit later."

White will have two extra pawns and will push them through more or less as demonstrated in Diagram 300. The reason for White's easy success is that he created not merely a passed pawn but an *outside passed pawn* (when there is more than one passed pawn, we say that the one farthest away from the main action is the outside passed pawn). The outside passed pawn acted as a decoy that lured the opponent's King out of action, thereby permitting the White monarch to mop up.

A common scenario when a passed pawn begins its promotion-run is that the weaker side sacrifices material to prevent Queening (the threat is often enough to force a sacrifice), and the stronger side uses his advantage in force to promote another pawn or to pursue the enemy King. In the next position, both sides have equal material, but White already has a passed pawn at c6, which is imbued with what Aron Nimzovich, a great player of the 1920s and 30s, called "a lust to expand" or to advance to the Queening square.

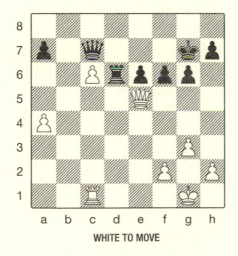

DIAGRAM 305

WHITE TO MOVE

When making a plan, White needs to establish a goal, which in this case is to Queen the c-pawn on c8. "My pawn," White ought to say to himself, "is blocked by Black's Queen. But the Black Queen is also performing a second task: It is guarding the Rook on d6. There's the answer! I can decoy the Black Queen off c7 by sacrificing with 1. Qxd6, forcing 1. ... Qxd6 in reply. Then I play 2. c7. Black cannot stop me from playing 3. c8=Q unless he gives up his Queen for the pawn. I finish up a Rook and win easily."

In many positions the side with a passed pawn must establish direct control over the Queening square to win, which is a consideration that should always be present when planning the advance of a passed pawn. In the previous example, if Black had been able to stick his Queen on c8, then White would have been down a Queen for a Rook. Chess wags say that failing to control the Queening square can result (to borrow a football phrase) in a "sack of the passer."

The question of whether a pawn will promote and cost the other side decisive material when capturing the new Queen is often decided by no more than a single move.

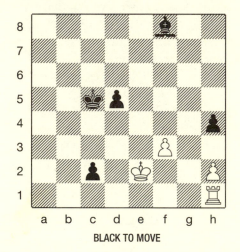

DIAGRAM 306

BLACK TO MOVE

In the above position, White would actually have good winning chances with 1. Rc1, menacing the unstoppable 2. Rxc2+. But with Black to move, the game is effectively over after 1. ... Bh6, taking control of c1 and menacing 2. ... c1=Q 3. Rxc1 Bxc1, finishing up a piece. Notice that after 1. ... Bh6 the White King cannot effectively approach the pawn because d2 is covered by the Bishop and d1 by the pawn.

The third consideration when advancing a passed pawn is to make sure that if there is a race going on, you promote your pawn first. In 90-plus percent of endgames, the side that promotes a pawn first also wins the game.

Victory, then, is to the swift. And this often means counting moves to see which side Queens first. Here is perhaps the most famous instance in all chess history of a great player forgetting to count from one to three:

ROBERT FISCHER–RENE LETELIER
MAR DEL PLATA, 1959

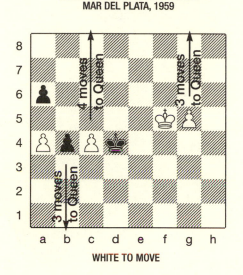

DIAGRAM 307

WHITE TO MOVE

The player with White is none other than the American chess genius Robert Fischer, official world champion of the International Chess Federation from 1972 to 1975, and the man whom many chess aficionados also regard as the "real champion" at least until 1985 when Kasparov assumed the crown. Many chess observers also believe that Fischer is the greatest player ever.

In the above position, White has passed c- and g-pawns, while Black has a b-passer. The reader can see that Fischer's g-pawn is three moves away from promotion and his c-pawn four moves away, while Black's b-pawn is three. So, Bobby pushes the g-pawn, right?

Wrong! In the worst single blunder of his illustrious career, Fischer the Great inexplicably fails to count moves.

    1.   c5??

Correct is 1. g6 b3 2. g7 b2 3. g8=Q b1=Q+ with a probable draw. In this line Fischer does not win even though he makes a first Queen because Black Queens with a check.

    1.   ...   b3

Imagine the pleasant shock that 1. c5?? gave Fischer's strong Chilean opponent, who wastes no time in obeying the injunction that passed pawns are meant to be pushed.

    2.   c6   b2

| 3. | c7 | b1=Q+ |

Check! Now Black stops White from Queening.

| 4. | Ke6 | Qb7 |

Black establishes control over the Queening square.

| 5. | Kd7 | Kd5 |
| 6. | g6 | |

If White tries to make a Queen by 6. Kd8 (to remove the pin by Black's Queen), he gets mated after 6. ... Kd6 7. c8=Q Qe7.

6.	...	Qc6+
7.	Kd8	Qd6+
	White resigns	

The likely conclusion is 8. Kc8 (to keep the c-pawn) 8. ... Kc6 9. Kb8 Qxc7+ 10. Ka8 Qb7 mate.

We have looked at three devices to achieve the first goal of endgame strategy, which is to transform a passed pawn into a Queen. These devices are:

· Eliminate or decoy away enemy pieces or pawns blocking the passer's advance.

· Establish, when necessary, control over the Queening square.

· Count moves in endgames where both sides have passed pawns and are in a race.

The second goal of endgame strategy is to exploit a material advantage that is sufficient to force checkmate. In the endgame, there are four well known instances of material advantage that the superior side cannot win:

· The stronger side is unable to mate in King + Bishop vs. King endings no matter how poorly the man with the lone monarch may play. Mate is not possible.

· Ditto King + Knight vs. King.

· The stronger side is unable to force mate in King + Two Knights vs. King, if the weaker party plays reasonably.

- King + Rook pawn (a- or h-pawn) vs. King is a draw. It does not matter how many a- or h-pawns one may have; the King of the weaker side cannot be driven from the Queening square, which means conversely that the stronger side is unable to gain control of the Queening square.

As the play from Diagram 308 demonstrates, the weaker party in King + Rook pawn vs. King endings can hold a draw by keeping his King in the relevant corner.

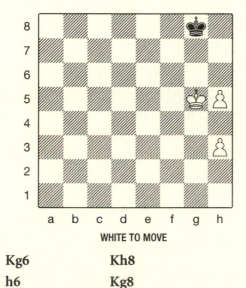

DIAGRAM 308

WHITE TO MOVE

1.	Kg6	Kh8
2.	h6	Kg8

Whatever White does, Black need only shift his King back and forth between h8 and g8.

3.   h4

On 3. h7+ Kh8, Black is suddenly stalemated, and White must surrender the pawn if he wishes to keep the game going.

3.   ...   Kh8

Life is easy, life is good, comrades.

4.   h5   Kg8

White's last two pawn moves are absolutely pointless. We are merely showing for effect that Black need only move his King back and forth, back and forth.

5.   h7+   Kh8

6.   Kh6 stalemate

The key rule of thumb in exploiting a material advantage sufficient to checkmate is that when you are a pawn or two ahead, seek exchanges of pieces rather than pawns. Conversely, if a pawn behind, seek exchanges of pawns rather than pieces.

Do you see the logic behind this rule of thumb? Many players find themselves in one of the four above-mentioned drawn endings because they exchanged too many pawns and at a given moment, the weaker party sacrificed his last piece for a pawn and reached, say, an ending of King vs. King + Knight.

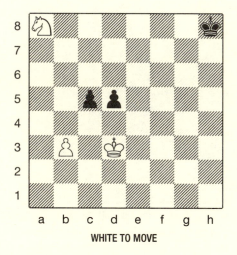

DIAGRAM 309

WHITE TO MOVE

Although White is up a piece, this ending is finely balanced. If Black were on move, he could force a draw immediately by 1. ... c4+ 2. bxc4 dxc4+ 3. Kxc4, when we reach an ending drawn by force.

Keeping in mind the strategic endgame goals of promoting a pawn to a Queen (including, to be sure, the creation of a passed pawn) and exploiting a material advantage sufficient to force mate, White needs to formulate a plan in Diagram 309 that will accomplish all three goals if he is to win.

"Okay," the first player says to himself, "I need to preserve my own pawn, or the King + Knight vs. King ending is drawn. Which means that I must first move my King and then use the Knight to attack and capture at least one of the pawns before the Black King arrives on the scene. Once I win his pawns, I've created a passer and will push it on to Queen."

That's the plan.

1. Kc3   Kg7

Black has nothing better. If 1. ... c4, then 2. b4, with a Queen promotion four moves away and the Black King five moves away. And if 1. ... d4+, then 2. Kc4, followed by 3. Nb6, 4. Na4 and 5. Nxc5, creating a passed pawn and inevitably winning the d-pawn.

2.	Nc7	d4+
3.	Kc4	Kf6
4.	Na6	Kf5

If 4. Kxc5, Black plays 4. ... d3, forcing White to find 5. Nb5 (5. Nd5+ also wins) 5. ... Ke5 (or 5. ... d2) 6. Nc3. White arranges to trade his Knight for the d-pawn and prepares to advance his b-pawn for a coronation on b8.

5.	Nxc5	Ke5
6.	b4	

Passed pawns are meant to be pushed. Another rule of thumb: When in doubt about what to do in a given endgame, and if you have a passed pawn, play the odds and advance it.

6.	...	Kd6
7.	Kxd4	

White will Queen his passed pawn and checkmate according to the method given later in this chapter.

ENDGAME PECULIARITIES

Certain types of endgame positions, which occur often enough to repay brief study, defy the common sense of a first glance. Earlier, we learned that King + Rook pawn vs. King was a draw. So, too, is King + Rook pawn + Bishop vs. King, if the Bishop is on the opposite color of the Queening square.

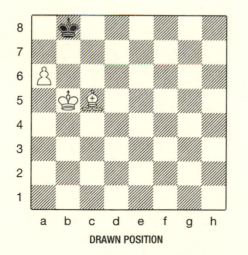

DIAGRAM 310

DRAWN POSITION

Black can draw the above position effortlessly for the same reason that he can draw the same ending without a Bishop: The stronger side cannot gain control of the Queening square. For example, on 1. Kb6, Black responds with 1. ... Ka8. If White attempts to control b8 with the pawn or Bishop, then it is stalemate.

A second species of endgame position that defies initial expectations occurs when one side has, say, two extra pawns, but each side also has a Bishop on squares of opposite color from the opponent's.

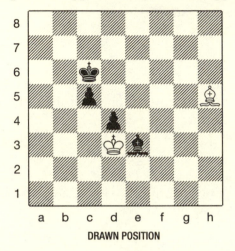

DIAGRAM 311

DRAWN POSITION

Although Black enjoys the big endgame advantage of two extra pawns, the game is a draw no matter who moves next. White need merely play Bf7, preventing the advance of the c-pawn; the game is hopelessly drawn. The key point is that because the Black Bishop is on dark squares, it cannot enforce any action on a light square such as c4. White's drawing technique will be never to touch his King and to shift his Bishop *ad infinitum* along the a2-g8 diagonal.

A third endgame peculiarity, occasionally seen in middlegames but far more often in endings, is that a single pawn (here White's g-pawn) can restrain two or three enemy pawns if properly posted.

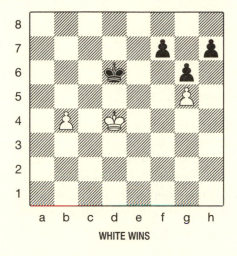

DIAGRAM 312

WHITE WINS

At first blush, Black must be winning, given his formidable array of King-side pawns. Not so. White has an elementary win no matter who is on move, for Black's Kingside array of three pawns is restrained by Black's single pawn. Let's give Black the first move:

1. ...	Ke6

There are two other doomed attempts at survival: (I.) 1. ... Kc6 (Black chases White's passed pawn and then tries to return to the Kingside in time) 2. Ke5 Kb5 3. Kf6 Kxb4 4. Kxf7 Kc5 5. Kg7 Kd5 6. Kxh7 Ke6 7. Kxg6 Ke7 8. Kh7 (taking control of the Queening square) 8. ... Kf8 9. g6, and White wins; and (II.) 1. ... f5 (Black stages a breakout; the other pawn move, 1. ... h5, is clearly hopeless, as White marches in for a Queen after 2. gxh6 *e.p.*) 2. gxf6 *e.p.* g5 (Black must try to run for a Queen) 3. f7 Ke7 4. b5 (White whipsaws the Black King with his widely separated passed pawns) 4. ... g4 5. Ke4 h5 6. Kf4, and White wins because he has stymied Black's Kingside pawns.

2. b5	

Passed pawns are meant to be pushed.

2. ...	f5

Black also loses after 2. ... Kd6, when White can choose from either (I) 3. b6 Kc6 4. Ke5 Kxb6 5. Kf6 Kc6 6. Kxf7 Kd6 7. Kg7 Ke6 8. Kxh7, when both 8. ... Kf7 and 8. ... Kf5 are met by 9. Kh6, winning the g-pawn and the game; or (II) 3. Kc4 Kd7 4. Kc5 Kc7 5. b6+ Kb7 6. Kb5 Kb8 7. Kc6 Kc8

8. b7+ Kb8 9. Kb6. Black's King has run out of moves, and the second player must move either his backward f- or h-pawn. A likely conclusion is 9. ... f5 10. gxf6 *e.p.* g5 11. f7 g4 12. f8=Q mate.

3.	gxf6 *e.p.*	g5
4.	b6	g4
5.	b7	g3
6.	b8=Q	g2
7.	Qg3 and White wins	

Endgame study can be useful for understanding other phases of the game because the raw characteristics of the pieces can be seen clearly. Rooks often have unhindered access along ranks and files. Knights hop about without being hobbled by friendly pieces on otherwise available squares. Queens swoop along uncluttered diagonals and from one end or side of the board to the other. Bishops slide along wide open diagonals. These liberated pieces may then perform tactical jobs seldom available in the middlegame.

DIAGRAM 313

WHITE TO MOVE

The game appears dead drawn no matter who is on move. With Black to move, he simply captures the passed b-pawn; since White cannot possibly checkmate Black with a single Bishop, White responds by capturing Black's pawn, removing any chance Black had of Queening a pawn as well. And if White is to move, he appears to have no way to prevent Black from capturing the b7 pawn.

The winning tactical device is 1. Bxc6, a type of decoy sacrifice seldom seen in middlegames. If Black recaptures with 1. ... Kxc6, then 2. b8=Q.

Notice that the same combination can be played if the whole position is moved down the board—for example, with the White pawn on d5, the Black pawn at e4, and the Black King at e5. Here, 1. Bxe4 is still a winner.

This combination is effective not because of how close the b-pawn is to Queening, but because the White pawn wins any race where the Black King is a rank behind. This particular decoy tactic can be executed by every piece except the King. For example, in Diagram 313, imagine that White has a Knight on f5 instead of a Bishop on f3, and remove Black's pawn at c6. Then, 1. Nd6 wins because taking the Knight allows 2. b8=Q+.

BASIC ENDGAME MATES

The mate involving King + Two Rooks vs. King is called the *lawnmower* because the two Rooks mow down the King row by row until it is mated along the edge. First, the stronger side cuts off the board from the opponent's King; second, the King is forced to the edge of the board and mated. A typical position:

DIAGRAM 314

WHITE TO MOVE AND FORCE MATE

1. **Ra4**

Called "building a fence." The Black King is confined to half of the board.

1. ...   **Kd5**
2. **Rb5+**

Beginning the mowing process, row by row, and forcing the Black King ever closer to the board's edge.

2. ...   **Kc6**
3. **Rh5**

On 3. Ra6+, Black captures the b5 Rook. The time has come to zip a Rook over to the other side of the board, a common ploy in the lawnmower.

3. ...   **Kd6**

Trying his darndest.

    4.   Ra6+

Of course, 4. Rg4, followed by 5. Rg6+, also gets the job done eventually. White has many ways to win.

4.	...	Kc7
5.	Rh7+	Kb8
6.	Rg6	Kc8
7.	Rg8 mate	

A second basic mate is King + Queen and Rook vs. King. This mate is more easily executed than even the two-Rook lawnmower. If the Rook on a2 in Diagram 314 becomes a Queen, there is no need for the Queen and Rook to switch to the other side of the board. Since the Queen protects the Rook, the winning moves are 1. Qa4, 2. Rb5+, 3. Qa6+, 4. Rb7+ and 5. Qa8 mate—regardless of what Black does.

    A third basic mate is King + Rook vs. King.

DIAGRAM 315

WHITE TO MOVE AND FORCE MATE

With correct play, White has no problem in forcing mate. Since the position is completely won for the stronger side, it makes no difference who moves first. White forces the game by:

1. Deciding on which edge he wishes to drive the Black King. (Let's make it the eighth rank.)

2. Cutting off the Black King from the first four ranks.

3. Centralizing his King, which in cooperation with the Rook can drive the enemy King to the eighth rank.

Let's see how it's done. In this sequence we reintroduce you to the concept of the waiting move (for more information, see the explanation and example starting on page 213).

> **1.   Rh4**

Suddenly, the Black King is confined to the upper half of the board.

> **1.   ...   Ke5**

> **2.   Kb2**

Now comes centralization of the King, who will work in conjunction with the Rook to corral the Black King on the eighth rank.

> **2.   ...   Kd5**

> **3.   Kc3   Ke5**

Black is staying in the center as far from the edge as possible. Other moves are worse.

> **4.   Rd4**

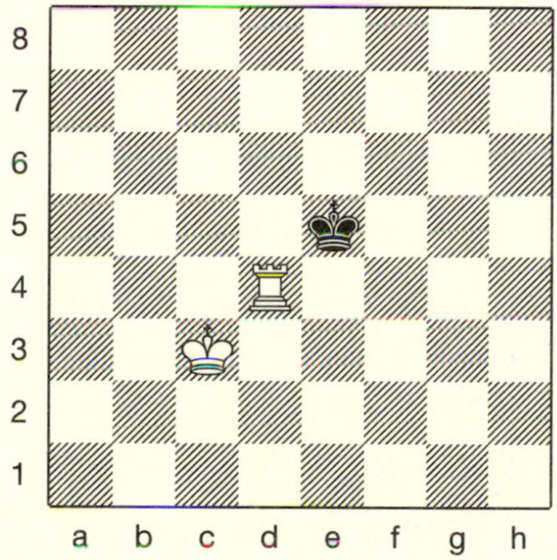

DIAGRAM 316

Now the Black King is cut off from the Queenside and confined to one-quarter of the board. Notice how the White King protects the Rook, an example of piece cooperation.

> **4.   ...   Kf5**

> **5.   Kd3   Ke5**

> **6.   Ke3**

A key moment. Many beginners play a move like 6. Re4+, which allows the Black King to escape to the Queenside with 6. ... Kd5, thereby lengthening the mating process.

> **6.   ...   Kf5**

The Black King is in *zugzwang* and must leave the center. No better is 6. ... Ke6 7. Kf4 Kf6 8. Rd6+ Ke7 9. Ke5 and so on.

7.   Re4   Kf6

If 7. ... Kg5, then 8. Rf4 cuts off the King from the f-file.

8.   Kf4   Kg6

White takes over f5 and g5. But if Black could pass and not make a move, he would not lose. This "but" is another word for *zugzwang*.

9.   Re6+

Forcing Black to the seventh rank, since 9. ... Kh5 is met by a Rook waiting moving along the sixth rank—for example, 10. Ra6 Kh4 (the only legal move) 11. Rh6 mate.

9.   ...   Kf7

10.   Kf5   Kg7

11.   Re7+   Kf8

Black had to go to the eighth rank because 11. ... Kh6 is met by 12. Rf7 Kh5 (in *zugzwang* again) 13. Rh7 mate.

12.   Kf6   Kg8

13.   Kg6

An equally efficient mating method is to make a waiting move along the seventh rank such as 13. Ra7, forcing 13. ... Kh8 (if 13. ... Kf8, then 14. Ra8 mate) 14. Kg6 Kg8 15. Ra8 mate.

13.   ...   Kf8

DIAGRAM 317

14.   Re1

A waiting move along the e-file. Also possible are such waiting moves as 14. Re6, 14. Re5 and so on.

14.	...	Kg8
15.	**Re8 mate**	

Most King and Rook mates can be done between 15 and 20 moves, well short of the 50-move draw rule. At first, you will most likely not drive the King to the edge in the most efficient manner. That is not too important, if once you have the King on the edge, you understand the above waiting-move method to force checkmate.

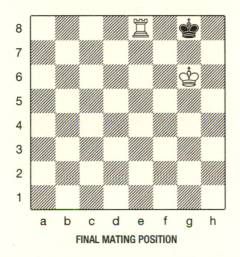

DIAGRAM 318

FINAL MATING POSITION

The fourth basic mating position covered in this chapter involves King + Queen vs. King. Although the Queen needs its own King to force check-mate, it can drive the enemy monarch to the edge of the board without aid. Once again, the process involves cutting off the board and mating along the edge.

DIAGRAM 319

WHITE TO MOVE AND FORCE MATE

1.   **Qf4**

Right off the bat, White denies Black half of the board.

1.	...	Ke6
2.	Qg5	Kd6
3.	Qf5	Kc6
4.	Qe5	Kb6
5.	Qd5	

The Queen confines the King without giving a single check, always staying a Knight's move away from the Black King, which, unable to attack the Queen, is forced to give ground.

5.	...	Kc7
6.	Qe6	Kb7
7.	Qd6	Kc8

White relentlessly forces Black to the edge.

8.	Qe7	Kb8

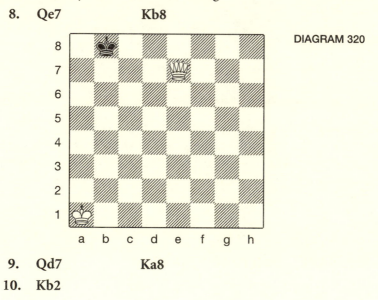

DIAGRAM 320

9.	Qd7	Ka8
10.	Kb2	

We hope and trust that you were not expecting 10. Qc7. That is stalemate, not checkmate!

10.	...	Kb8

Black is reduced to shifting his King between a8 and b8. The concluding moves could be:

11.	Kb3	Ka8
12.	Kb4	Kb8
13.	Kb5	Ka8

14.	**Kb6**	**Kb8**
15.	**Qb7 mate**	

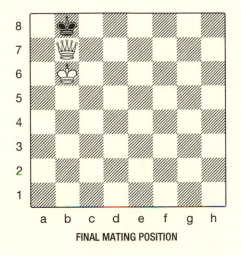

DIAGRAM 321

FINAL MATING POSITION

MAIN ENDGAME CHARACTERISTICS

1. Forces are reduced. Queens are usually gone.

2. Material advantages loom larger than in the opening or middlegame.

3. The King becomes a fighting piece and should be centralized.

4. Pawns grow in relative importance, especially against Bishops and Knights.

5. It is sometimes desirable not to make a move. (See page 212 for a discussion of *zugzwang*.)

DRAWN ENDINGS WITH UNEQUAL MATERIAL

1. King + Bishop vs. King.

2. King + Knight vs. King.

3. King + Two Knights vs. King. Unlike numbers 1 and 2, this type of mate is theoretically possible, but it cannot be forced from a normal starting position.

4. King + Rook Pawn vs. King when the enemy King is in front of the pawn.

5. King + Bishop + Rook Pawn vs. King when the Bishop is on squares of opposite color from the Queening square.

BASIC ENDGAME STRATEGY

1. Create a passed pawn.

2. Promote this passed pawn to a Queen.

3. Use your material advantage to force checkmate.

BASIC STEPS TO PROMOTE A PASSED PAWN

1. When necessary, eliminate enemy pieces or pawns blocking the pawn's progress.

2. When necessary, establish control over the Queening square.

3. In the event of a race between a passed pawn on each side, calculate who promotes first.

CHESS MOVIE: IRRESISTIBLE FORCE MEETS MOVABLE OBJECT

Here we present a game decided in the ending. Robert Fischer is a virtuoso performer in the endgame, making the murky appear clear and the complicated simple. In this game as White, his treatment of the ending involves a single, simple, seemingly unstoppable idea: He creates a central pawn mass, pushes it forward, and attacks the Black King trying to impede the advance. Pawn play of the highest order! Conducting Black is Argentina's Jorge Rubinetti, who in the path of Fischer's irresistible force proves to be an eminently movable object. The scene is the Buenos Aires International of 1970, and the opening moves leading to Diagram 322 are 1. e4 e5 2. Nf3 Nc6 3. Bb5 a6 4. Bxc6 dxc6 5. 0-0.

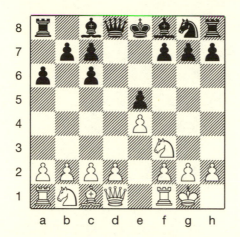

DIAGRAM 322

1. The endgame commences quickly after 5. ... f6 6. d4 Bg4 7. dxe5 Qxd1 8. Rxd1, which produces a well known position from the Exchange Variation of the Ruy Lopez. Fischer employs a virtuoso technique in this apparently dry ending—suggestive of Sviatoslav Richter playing Bach's "Goldberg Variations."

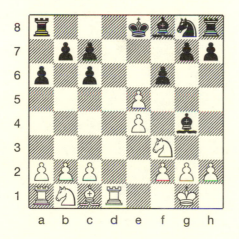

DIAGRAM 323

2. Black decides to weaken White's pawns and to go for a full-fledged ending after 8. ... Bxf3 9. gxf3 fxe5. White's edge is slight—a possibility of creating a passed pawn on the e-file. Black has little chance of creating a passed pawn on the Queenside because of his doubled c-pawns.

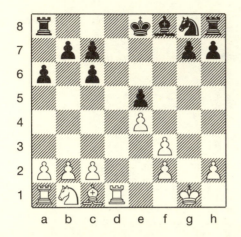

DIAGRAM 324

3. An interlude. Both players position their pieces: 10. Be3 Bd6 11. Nd2. Fischer selects d2 for his Knight because from the seemingly more active c3, the Knight has little future at a4, b5 or d5. But after Nd2, then Nc4 followed by Na5 is a real possibility.

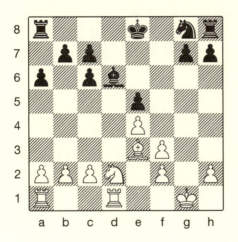

DIAGRAM 325

4. Fischer and Rubinetti continue to build up in and around the center: 11. ... Ne7 12. Nc4 0-0-0 13. Rd3. One point to 13. Rd3 is 13. ... Ng6 14. Bg5 Rd7 15. Rad1 h6 16. Nxd6+ cxd6 17. Rxd6 Rxd6 18. Rxd6 hxg5 19. Rxg6, winning a second pawn. See Diagram 327 for the other point.

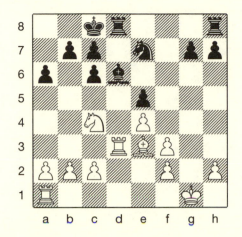

DIAGRAM 326

5. Black must chase the Knight off c4 or face such threats as Rad1 and Nxd6, when White wins a pawn. If Black redeploys his Knight to g6, another threat for White is to pile up on the b-pawn by 14. Na5, with possibly 15. Rb3 b6 16. Nxc6 to follow. Hence 13. ... b5. The onus of accuracy is on Black to hold a draw.

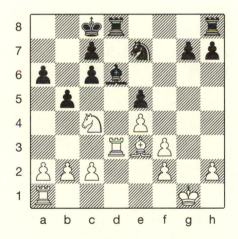

DIAGRAM 327

6. After 14. Na5 Bb4 (trying to dislodge the bone from his throat) 15. Nb3 (eyeing the a5 and c5 squares) 15. ... Rxd3 (to prevent White from doubling on the d-file) 16. cxd3 Ng6, White has pawns on the central d- and e-files. We suddenly see the second point behind Fischer's 13. Rd3.

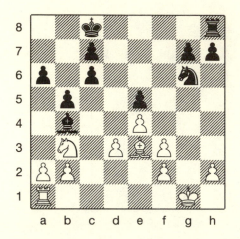

DIAGRAM 328

7. Before the d- and f-pawns can start rolling, they need backup protection. Fischer plays 17. Kf1, and Rubinetti replies with 17. ... Rf8 (attacking the f-pawn) 18. Ke2 Nf4+. The alternative is 18. ... Nh4 19. Rg1 Rf7 20. Rg3 when White has some hope to get his central pawns moving.

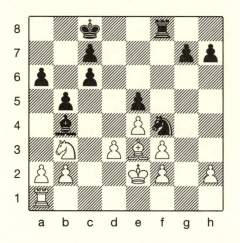

DIAGRAM 329

8. White takes off the Knight by 19. Bxf4 Rxf4 and then plays 20. Rg1, attacking the pawn on g7. The critical juncture: Black should defend with 20. ... g6 21. Rg4 but instead counterattacks by 20. ... Rh4, hoping to offset White's central pawn surge by advancing his h-pawn.

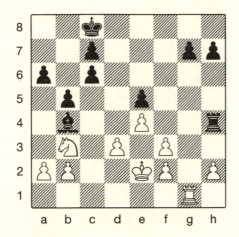

DIAGRAM 330

9. Fischer believes in central control and does not hesitate: 21. Rxg7 Rxh2 22. a3 Bd6. Material remains even, and Black has a pawn on h7 waiting to sprint down the outside lane. Yet, it will never move. Black's Rook on h2 is far from the action, and White creates one threat after another, starting with ...

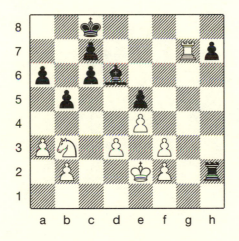

DIAGRAM 331

10. 23. f4!—Fischer's resource. The threat is 24. f5, followed by 25. f6, and onward to the eighth rank. Rubinetti is forced to play 23. ... exf4, removing his guard from the d4-square. Although temporarily up a pawn, Black is now quite lost. Here comes the White horde.

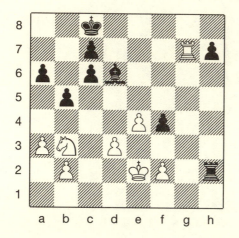

DIAGRAM 332

11. White pushes forward with 24. d4, intending 25. e5 Bf8 26. Rg8, pinning and winning the Bishop. Black must therefore venture his King toward the center to support the Bishop and to struggle against White's two center pawns. The move is 24. ... Kd8, and it endangers the Black King.

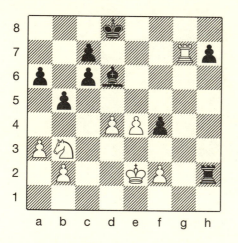

DIAGRAM 333

12. White plays 25. Na5, attacking the pawn on c6 and bringing up another piece to harass the King and to support the central pawn advance. Black strikes at the pawn center with 25. ... c5, an effort to hinder the White pawn horde. But he who sins strategically cannot be redeemed tactically.

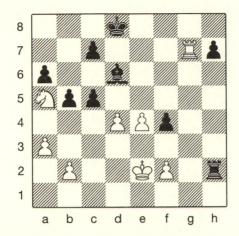

DIAGRAM 334

13. The right idea now is to push straight ahead with 26. e5, forcing Black to play 26. ... Bf8. Simple endgame chess: Fischer grabs the center and plows forward. Yet many lesser players might have dithered and delayed the central attack, giving Black a chance to recover.

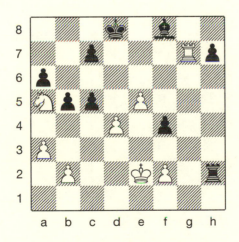

DIAGRAM 335

14. White checks with 27. Nc6+, and Black flees by 27. ... Ke8. He wants to save the Bishop at f8 which would be lost after 27. ... Kc8 28. Rg8 Kb7 29. d5 because if the Bishop moves then White has 30. Rb8 mate. But mate is on the docket in spite of the reduced forces.

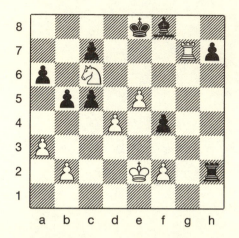

DIAGRAM 336

15. The end nears. White plays 28. Rxc7. The threat is 29. e6 and 30. Rc8 mate. Fischer's supreme self-confidence is shown by his employing the simplest means—no backing and filling, just pushing forward in the serene expectation that the few pieces at his command will prove sufficient.

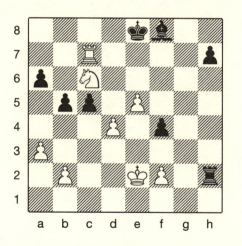

DIAGRAM 337

16. The end comes. Black resigns. The defense, 28. ... Rh6, is crushed by 29. d5, intending 30. e6 and 31. Rc8 mate. Fischer often won by pursuing a simple idea like centralization. As with Vince Lombardi's Green Bay Packers, opponents knew what to expect but could not prevent it.

CHAPTER

10 *Chessercizes for Energetic Endings*

Endgame characteristics, strategy, tactics and checkmates are the subjects of this test chapter. Keep in mind that in many endgames, it is the meek pawns that are slated to inherit the chess earth, which means that while most pawns are weak compared with pieces in middlegames, they can transform themselves into Queens in endgames.

Many of these chessercizes have as key themes the creation of passed pawns, their advance forward to promotion, control of the Queening square, use of the King as a fighting piece, and maintenance of sufficient material to force checkmate. The rule of thumb about keeping pawns and trading pieces when up material will figure in several questions. Stalemates, the chessic equivalent of Revenge of the Nerds, are also lurking here and there.

In many instances, you will enjoy overwhelming superiority and need "merely" apply endgame strategy as outlined in Chapter 9. When studying the positions, try to employ the relevant portions of the analytical method provided on page 161. Unlike many middlegame positions in which the goals are manifold, you already know that the goal in many of these endgame positions is to promote a pawn or force a checkmate with limited material.

When working through the test, just examine the pieces in each diagram, answer the question and check your answer at the bottom of the page or on the following page. If your answer is wrong or, still worse, if you fail to understand why it is wrong, then review the relevant portion of Chapter 9 or earlier chapters.

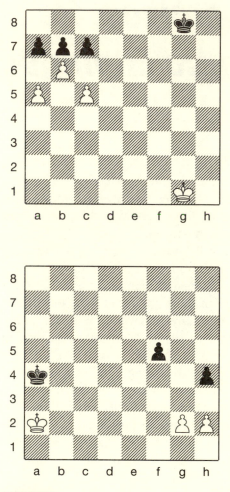

DIAGRAM 338

1. What did White hope to gain by playing 1. b6?

DIAGRAM 339

2. With Black to move, is 1. ... f4 or 1. ... h3 the better way to create a passed pawn?

ANSWERS

1. A passed pawn destined for Queening. After 1. b6, White menaces either bxa7 or bxc7, Queening next move. But Black appears able to defend against this idea by capturing on b6 with either his a- or c-pawn. For example, after 1. ... axb6, there is no passed pawn after 2. cxb6 cxb6 3. axb6. However, after 1. ... axb6, White can continue with 2. c6, forcing 2. ... bxc6, and now the passer appears with 3. a6. White wins. If Black varies with 1. ... cxb6, White plays 2. a6 bxa6 3. c6 Kf7 4. c7 Ke7 5. c8=Q, winning. Remember: If the conditions are right, pawn breaks can produce passed pawns.

2. Neither is "the better way." On 1. ... h3, White answers 2. g3. On 1. ... f4, menacing 2. ... h3 3. g3 f3, White can defend against this threat with 2. h3.

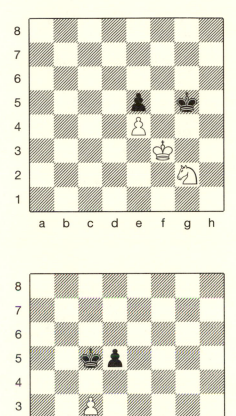

DIAGRAM 340

3. With White to move, describe his strategy. Give a winning line for White.

DIAGRAM 341

4. Is 1. Nd1 or 1. Kd3 the better move for White?

ANSWERS

3. White's strategy is to create a passed pawn by winning Black's pawn, promote his passer to a Queen, and checkmate Black. There are many ways for White to accomplish his tasks, including 1. Ne1 Kf6 2. Nd3 (attacking the pawn and forcing Black to keep a King guard on the foot soldier) 2. ... Ke6 3. Kg4 Kf6 4. Kh5 Ke6 (Black is forced to give way, another example of *zugzwang*) 5. Kg6 Kd6 6. Kf6 Kd7 7. Nxe5+. White has won Black's pawn and will soon crown his passer on e8.

4. On 1. Nd1, Black forces the exchange of pawns by 1. ... d4. The stronger side must maintain sufficient mating material, which can be done with 1. Kd3. White will eventually win Black's d-pawn and Queen his own c-pawn.

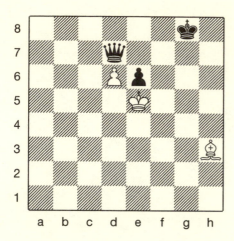

DIAGRAM 342

5. With White to move, who stands better?

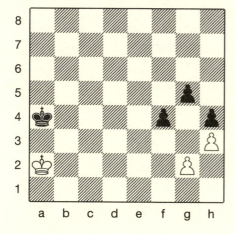

DIAGRAM 343

6. With Black to move, can he create a passed pawn? With White to move, what is the outcome?

DIAGRAM 344

7. With Black to move, what is the outcome? With White to move?

ANSWERS

5. White can force a passed pawn and win the game by 1. Bxe6+ Qf7 (if
   1. ... Qxe6+, then 2. Kxe6 Kf8 3. d7 and 4. d8=Q) 2. d7 Kf8 (the
   Queen is pinned) 3. Bxf7, and Black can't halt the pawn (3. ... Ke7 4.
   Be8 or 3. ... Kxf7 4. d8=Q).

6. Black wins no matter who is on move. If Black moves first, the process
   of creating a passed pawn is comparatively simple: 1. ... g4 (intending
   2. ... gxh3 3. gxh3 f3) 2. hxg4 f3 3. gxf3 h3, and Black wins. If White
   moves first, he at least has a fighting chance to run his King toward the
   pawns by 1. Kb2 g4 2. Kc2 (the old college try based on 2. ... gxh3? 3.
   gxh3 f3 4. Kd2 f2 5. Ke2, when White "sacks the passer") 2. ... f3! 3.
   Kd2 (there is nothing better; for example, 3. gxf3 gxh3 or 3. hxg4
   fxg2) 3. ... fxg2, Queening the pawn on the next move.

7. With Black to move, the game is drawn after 1. ... f4, threatening to
   trade off the last pawns, leaving a drawn King + Bishop vs. King ending. On 2. e4, Black simply plays 2. ... Kxe4. Which suggests that with
   White to move first, he can win by 1. Bb7 (or 1. Bd3), controlling e4
   after 1. ... f4 2. e4. Black loses his pawn after 2. ... Kf6 3. Kf2 Kg6 4. Kf3
   Kg5 5. Bc6, a waiting move that forces Black to move his King and lose
   the pawn. White then promotes his pawn to a Queen and checkmates
   Black. This example shows the importance of keeping sufficient mating material on the board.

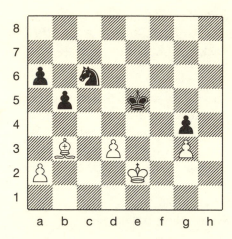

DIAGRAM 345

8. Who wins after Black plays 1. ... Nd4+?

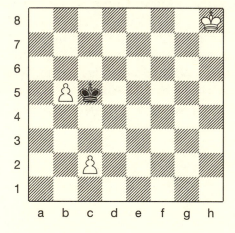

DIAGRAM 346

9. How should the game end with Black to play? With White to play?

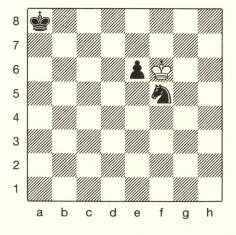

DIAGRAM 347

10. Why did Black choose 1. ... Nd4 over 1. ... Ng7?

ANSWERS

8. *Black can win because he creates an outside passed pawn. After 1. ... Nd4+, White realizes that Black intends to trade Knight for Bishop and then push his Queenside pawns. So, he runs for the Queen's wing with 2. Kd2, but he still loses: 2. ... Nxb3+ 3. axb3 a5 4. Kc3 a4 5. bxa4 bxa4 6. Kb4 Kd4 7. Kxa4 Kxd3 8. Kb3 Ke3 9. Kc2 Kf3 10. Kd2 Kxg3 11. Ke2 Kh2, followed by Queening the g-pawn. Notice how White's King had to jump offside to chase Black's passed a-pawn, thereby allowing the second player to clean house on the Kingside.*

9. *With Black to play, the game is drawn after 1. ... Kxb5 2. Kg7 Kc4 3. Kf6 Kc3 4. Ke5 Kxc2. With White to play, he wins with 1. c4. Note that Black cannot capture the c-pawn. A general rule is that the side with a protected passed pawn (the pawn on c4 protects the one on b5) in King-and-pawn endings usually wins.*

10. *Black chose 1. ... Nd4 over 1. ... Ng7 because he did not know what he was doing! After 1. ... Nd4, White draws by 2. Ke5 with a double attack on Knight and pawn. When the Knight moves, White captures the pawn, reaching a drawn King + Knight vs. King ending. On the other hand 1. ... Ng7 protects the pawn, and if White tries 2. Kxg7, then Black wins the Queening race by 2. ... e5. In many pared-down end-games, it is better to protect a passed pawn from behind than in front because if the opponent's King captures the defender behind, it loses the Queening race.*

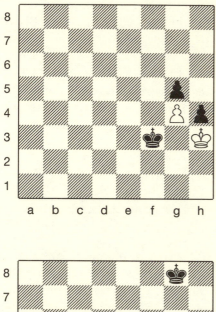

DIAGRAM 348

11. With White to move, he is in *zugzwang*. But what happens if Black moves first?

DIAGRAM 349

12. Can Black play and win?

ANSWERS

11. White's only move is 1. Kh2, when Black captures with 1. ... Kxg4. Yet with Black to move, White is still in *zugzwang* after 1. ... Kf4. Notice that Black's 1. ... Kf4, which does nothing in itself, is nonetheless a winner because it forces White to move. In the middlegame, most waiting moves are actually losing moves that permit the opponent to develop his game, but waiting moves in the endgame are frequently the offspring of deep strategy.

12. Yes, with 1. ... Be5. On 2. Kxe5, Black wins the Queening derby after 2. ... f3; if White eschews the capture, then Black advances his King and eventually Queens the passer. Yet another example of why passed pawns should usually be protected from behind.

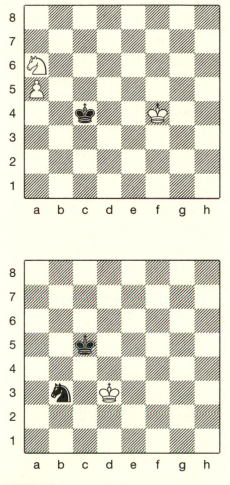

DIAGRAM 350

13. With White to move, can he Queen his pawn?

DIAGRAM 351

14. If you were White, could world champion Garry Kasparov defeat you if he moves first?

ANSWERS

13. Yes, with 1. Nb4 Kb5 2. a6, and we have another case of the passed pawn protected from behind. Compare this example with that in Chessercize 10, and notice that protection from the side (1. Nc5 Kxc5 2. a6 Kb6 3. a7 Kxa7) or from the front (1. Nb8 Kb5 2. a6 Kb6 3. Ke5 Ka7 4. Kd6 Kxb8 and 1. Nc7 Kc5 2. a6 Kb6 3. Ke5 Kxc7 4. a7 Kb7) is inadequate to win.

14. No. World champion Garry Kasparov could not checkmate an unnerved hummingbird in this position because it is physically impossible to construct a mating position with King + Knight vs. King.

DIAGRAM 352

15. Is this position—King + Rook pawn vs. King—a dead draw?

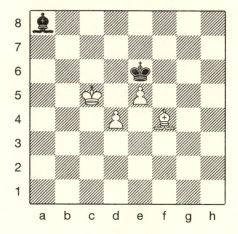

DIAGRAM 353

16. What happens with White to move first? With Black to move first?

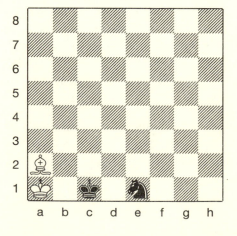

DIAGRAM 354

17. Are there realistic winning chances for either side?

ANSWERS

15. No. Because Black can establish control over the mating square by 1. ... Kb2, and White can do nothing to prevent a coronation after 2. Kd3 a4 3. Kc4 a3, and so on. However, if White is on move, he can draw by 1. Kc1 Ka2 (Black must keep White out of the corner) 2. Kc2. If now 2. ... a4, then 3. Kc1 Ka1 4. Kc2 and so on.

16. The game is a dead draw, no matter who moves·first. Black need merely keep his King on e6 and slide his Bishop indefinitely along the h1-a8 diagonal. If 1. d5+, then Black captures with 1. ... Bxd5. White's problem is that his Bishop is on dark squares and cannot enforce the advance of the two extra pawns. In endgames where Bishops are on opposite-colored squares, the weaker side often has chances to draw the game as shown in this diagram. If each side had a Rook or other pieces in the diagrammed position, then White would try to keep his Rooks on the board, while Black would try to trade off to reach what chessplayers call a Bishops-of-opposite-color ending.

17. Were you alert? If White moves first, the game is a draw after any Bishop move; if Black moves first, he mates with 1. ... Nc2. True enough, endings of King + Knight vs. King are drawn perforce, but if the opponent also has a piece, then it is theoretically possible to construct a checkmate, though such a mate cannot be forced except in special positions like the one in this diagram.

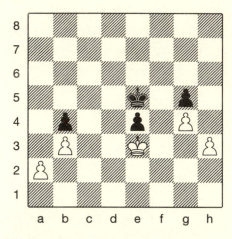

DIAGRAM 355

18. Who is winning this position? Either side to move.

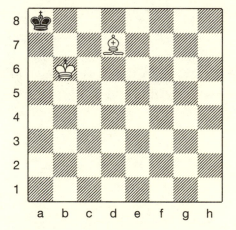

DIAGRAM 356

19. White to move. Can he win?

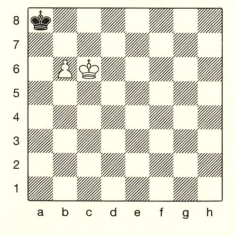

DIAGRAM 357

20. What happens if White is on move? If Black is on move?

ANSWERS

18. Black is a pawn down, but he is winning regardless of who moves first. Notice how Black's single b-pawn restrains two White pawns (if 1. a4, then 1. ... bxa3 *e.p.*) and how his g-pawn is performing the same labor on the Kingside. If White moves first, the conclusion might be 1. h4 gxh4 2. g5 h3 3. g6 h2 (or 3. ... Kf6) 4. g7 h1=Q (remember our refrain: He who promotes first usually wins) 5. g8=Q Qe1 mate. The e-pawn guards the d3 and f3 escape squares in the same fashion as the d-pawn in Diagram 20 on page 27. If Black moves first, he wins by 1. ... Kd5 2. Ke2 (2. h4 fails against 2. ... gxh4 3. g5 h3 4. g6 Ke6, when Black catches the g-pawn and White cannot stop both the e- and h-pawns) 2. ... Kd4 3. Kd2 e3+ 4. Ke2 Ke4 5. Ke1 Kd3 6. Kd1 e2+ 7. Ke1 Ke3 (the position is not a stalemate because White still has pawn moves) 8. h4 gxh4 9. g5 h3 10. g6 h2 11. g7 h1=Q, with mate on the next move.

19. By now you know that Bobby Fischer could not checkmate an aard-vark in this position. It is physically impossible to construct a check-mate position in an ending of King + Bishop vs. King.

20. *Zugzwang*! Neither side wants to move first. If White moves, the game is a draw after either 1. b7+ Kb8 2. Kb6 stalemate or 1. Kb5 Kb7 2. Kc5 Kb8 3. Kc6 Kc8 4. b7+ Kb8 5. Kb6 stalemate. And if Black moves he loses very quickly after 1. ... Kb8 (the only legal move) 2. b7 Ka7 3. Kc7, when White has established control over the Queening square and will promote next move.

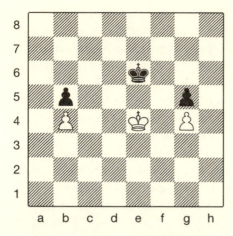

DIAGRAM 358

21. What happens if White moves first? If Black moves first?

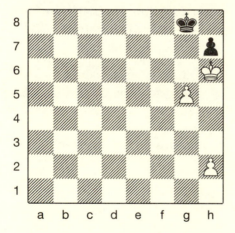

DIAGRAM 359

22. Is 1. h3 or 1. h4 the better move?

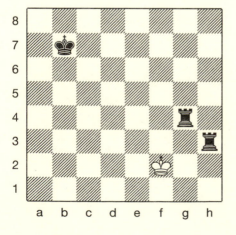

DIAGRAM 360

23. How can Black checkmate in four moves?

ANSWERS

21. *Zugzwang!* Neither side wants to move first. If White moves, the draw is obvious after 1. Kd4 Kd6 (to keep out the White King) 2. Ke4 Ke6 3. Kd4 Kd6 and so on. But if Black moves first, then he must let in the White King by 1. ... Kd6 2. Kf5 or by 1. ... Kf6 2. Kd5. White is the first to win a pawn and will also be the first to promote, well ahead of Black.

22. The better move is 1. h3 because of 1. ... Kh8 (Black is reduced to moving back and forth) 2. h4 Kg8 3. h5 Kh8 4. g6 hxg6 (if 4. ... Kg8, then 5. g7 Kf7 6. Kxh7, gaining control of the Queening square and promoting next move) 5. hxg6 Kg8 6. g7 Kf7 7. Kh7, and White promotes his pawn. But notice that if White plays 1. h4, the Black King is on h8 after 1. ... Kh8 2. h5 Kg8 3. g6 hxg6 4. hxg6 Kh8, and White has nothing better than 5. g7+ Kg8 6. Kg6 stalemate. The subtlety of losing a move by playing 1. h3 rather than 1. h4 is not properly meant for this introduction to chess, but we give it to show the complexity of chess even in positions with only a few pieces.

23. The lawnmower works after 1. ... Ra4 2. Kg2 Rb3 3. Kf2 Ra2+ 4. Ke1 Rb1 mate. After 1. ... Ra4, if White tries 2. Ke2, then 2. ... Ra2+ 3. Kf1 Rh1 mate. The move 1. ... Ra3 also gets the job done in four moves: (I.) 2. Ke2 Rg2+ 3. Kf1 Rb2 4. Ke1 Ra1 mate; or the shorter (II.) 2. Kf1 Ra2 3. Ke1 Rg1 mate.

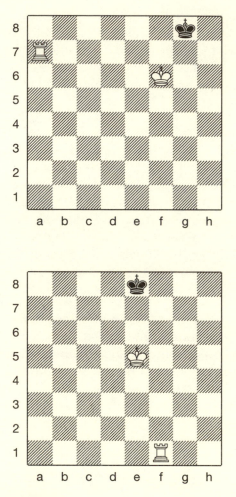

DIAGRAM 361

24. Can White checkmate in three moves?

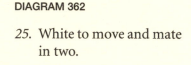

DIAGRAM 362

25. White to move and mate in two.

ANSWERS

24. Yes, in several ways. The most obvious idea is to play a waiting move such as 1. Rb7 (also 1. Rc7 or 1. Rd7) 1. ... Kh8 (if 1. ... Kf8, then 2. Rb8 mate) 2. Kg6 Kg8 3. Rb8 mate. Another idea is to play a waiting move along the a-file. For example, on 1. Ra2, it is mate after either 1. ... Kh7 2. Ra8 Kh6 3. Rh8 or 1. ... Kh8 2. Kf7 Kh7 3. Rh2. The only practical difficulty in administering checkmate with a King and a Rook is to remember how to use the device of the waiting move.

25. Black is threatening to escape to the seventh rank, and so a King move is in order to force mate in only two moves. Which is to say, 1. Kd6 Kd8 (the only legal move) 2. Rf8 mate.

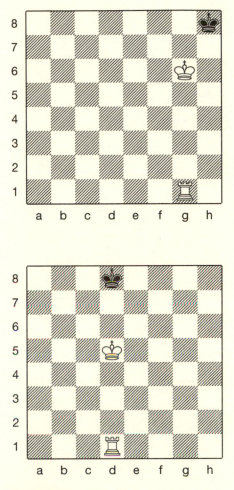

DIAGRAM 363

26. After 1. Kh6, what is Black's best continuation?

DIAGRAM 364

27. White to move and mate in three.

ANSWERS

26. To claim a draw by stalemate! Moving the King to the h-file uncovers the Rook on g1 and leaves Black without a move. Instead, White can checkmate in two moves by 1. Ra1 (moving the Rook to b1, c1, d1 or e1 works as well) 1. ... Kg8 2. Ra8 mate.

27. The problem with either 1. Kc6+ or 1. Ke6+ is that the Black King can escape to the seventh rank. The correct idea is 1. Kd6, leaving Black with two continuations, 1. ... Kc8 2. Rb1 Kd8 3. Rb8 mate or 1. ... Ke8 2. Rf1 Kd8 3. Rf8 mate.

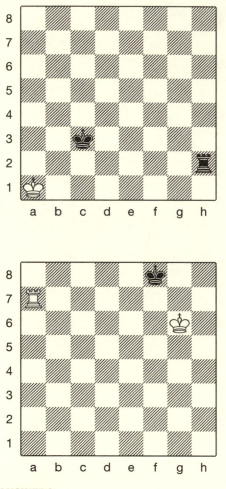

DIAGRAM 365

28. Does 1. ... Kb3 force mate more quickly than 1. ... Rb2?

DIAGRAM 366

29. White to move and force mate.

ANSWERS

28. Yes. White is in mate after 1. ... Kb3 2. Kb1 Rhl mate. There is a stale-mate after 1. ... Rb2.

29. There are several ways to force mate in this position. The most effi-cient way is 1. Kf6 Ke8 (if 1. ... Kg8, then 2. Rb7 Kh8 3. Kg6 Kg8 4. Rb8 mate) 2. Rh7 (this time around the waiting move is on the other side of the board) 2. ... Kd8 (if 2. ... Kf8, then 3. Rh8 mate) 3. Ke6 Kc8 4. Kd6 Kb8 5. Kc6 Ka8 6. Kb6 Kb8 7. Rh8 mate.

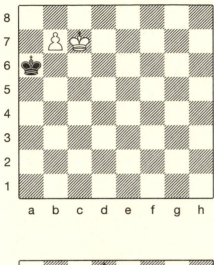

DIAGRAM 367

30. White to move and mate in three.

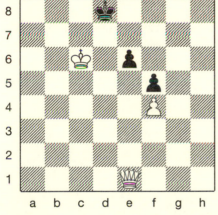

DIAGRAM 368

31. Which move, 1. Qxe6 or 1. Qe5, mates more quickly?

ANSWERS

30. The only challenge here is to give mate in no more than three moves: 1. b8=Q Ka5 2. Qb3! Ka6 3. Qb6 mate (or 3. Qa4 mate).

31. While 1. Qxe6 "looks" better and threatens 2. Qd7 mate, it also leaves Black in stalemate! A simple win is 1. Qe5 Ke7 2. Qg7+ Ke8 3. Kd6 e5 4. Qe7 mate.

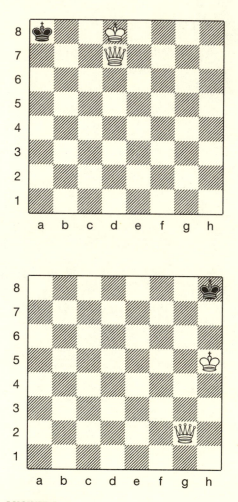

DIAGRAM 369

32. White to move and mate in two.

DIAGRAM 370

33. White to move and mate in two.

ANSWERS

32. We hope and trust that you did not answer with either 1. Kc8 stalemate or 1. Qc7 stalemate. Mate in two can be had by 1. Kc7 Ka7 2. Qa4 mate. This solution is the mirror image of the blunder in Chessercize 26. Here White masks the Queen to keep the Black King out of stalemate, and there White unmasked the Rook to put Black in stalemate.

33. Of course not 1. Kh6 stalemate or 1. Qg6 stalemate. The answer is 1. Kg6 Kg8 2. Qa8 mate.

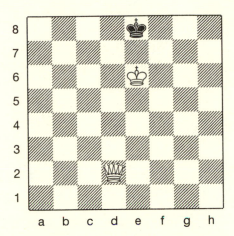

DIAGRAM 371

34. White to move and mate in two.

DIAGRAM 372

35. Black to move and mate in three.

ANSWERS

34. We are absolutely sure you found 1. Qd7+ Kf8 2. Qf7 mate or 1. Qd4 Kf8 2. Qh8 mate. Congratulate yourself! In this same type of position, world champion Garry Kasparov permitted a stalemate by 1. Qd6. There were extenuating circumstances: Kasparov was playing a wild and exciting speed game (both sides having only five minutes for the entire game) against a strong grandmaster, and in his eagerness to win he overlooked this stalemate pattern. Still, this mistake is probably the most elementary error in the champion's entire career.

35. If you moved your King to c5, c6 or c7, then you stalemated White! The correct continuation is 1. ... Qb3 2. Ka6 Kc6 3. Ka7 Qb7 mate.

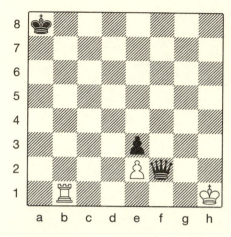

DIAGRAM 373

36. With White to move, what is the result?

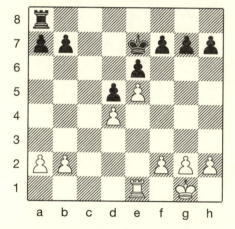

DIAGRAM 374

37. Does either side have winning chances if on move?

DIAGRAM 375

38. What happens if White is on move? If Black is on move?

ANSWERS

36. Did you notice that White's King would be in stalemate if he were without a Rook that can move? The drawing line is 1. Rb8+ Ka7 (remember: if 1. ... Kxb8, then it is stalemate) 2. Rb7+ Ka6 3. Rb6+ Ka5 4. Rb5+ and so on and on.

37. Do you remember our constant admonishments in Chapter 7 to place Rooks on open files in middlegames? The same is often true of endgames. In trying to develop a plan, both sides can see that material is dead even and that while White has a slight edge in space, he is behind in development with his King still stuck in the corner, while Black's monarch is in the center. Remember our call to centralize the King! A reasonable conclusion is that to win this game, it will be necessary to gain an advantage in material and that the only inroad for attack is the open c-file. If White plays 1. Rc1, Black is in a position to contest control of the file thanks to his centralized King, and after 1. ... Kd7 2. Kf1 Rc8 3. Rxc8 Kxc8, the position is very drawish. But if Black is on move, then he has excellent winning chances after 1. ... Rc8, threatening 2. ... Rc2 3. Rb1 Rd2, when he wins White's d-pawn. White would like to defend against this threat with 2. Re2, but this move is answered by 2. ... Rc1+, with a back-rank mate coming up. And if 2. Kf1 (trying to centralize the King), Black continues 2. ... Rc4 3. Rd1 Rc2 4. Rb1 Rd2, winning the d-pawn. The main difference in this ending is that Black has activated his King and White has not.

38. No matter who is on move, White wins the Queening race. Check out 1. ... Kg7 2. b5 Kf7 3. b6 Ke7 4. b7 Kd7 5. b8=Q. When White is on move, he outdistances Black even further. Practice counting moves and calculating who wins various King-and-pawn races.

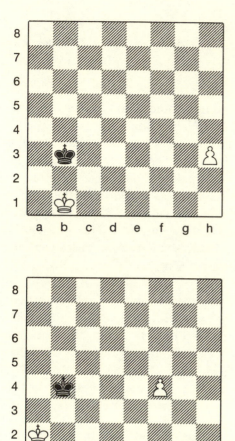

DIAGRAM 376

39. What happens if White is to move? If Black is to move?

DIAGRAM 377

40. What happens if White is to move? If Black plays 1. ... Kc3?

ANSWERS

39. If Black moves first, he can catch the pawn after 1. ... Kc3 2. h4 Kd4 3. h5 Ke5 4. h6 Kf6 5. h7 Kg7. If White moves first, Black falls one move short and loses the Queening race.

40. Even with White to move, he loses the Queening race after 1. f5 Kc5 2. f6 Kd6 3. f7 Ke7. But after 1. ... Kc3, which loses a rank, White is a full length ahead and wins the race by 2. f5 Kd4 3. f6 Ke5 4. f7 Ke6 5. f8=Q. Black blundered with 1. ... Kc3 because he wanted to bring his King one file closer to White's pawn but did not pay attention to losing a rank by moving from the fourth to the third.

11 *Using a Computer as a Chess Tutor*

PLAYING CHESS AGAINST A COMPUTER can provide endless hours of fun. At first, don't worry about the manifold uses of a chess computer; just keep playing against it, and you will learn from your mistakes by simply paying attention. But if you are eager to become better at the game, we have some suggestions that can turn any chess-playing program into an excellent tutor, though we will be recommending only two specific software programs for a home computer and a single dedicated chess computer from among the many good ones that are available. We believe that our recommendations combine excellent teaching features with a modest price.

As enthusiastic as we are personally about chess computers, we're also the first to admit that they may not be for everyone. Some people naturally learn better by reading books, taking classes from a chess teacher, or playing casually or in tournaments. We say: To each his own. Do whatever suits your individual study style.[1]

WHAT EQUIPMENT DO YOU NEED?

Our recommendations divide into two categories: chess software for a personal computer; and dedicated chess computers. See the list on page 271 for information on how to contact the companies mentioned in this chapter.

Chess Software. If you already own a home computer, the addition of chess playing software involves a relatively small investment, since one of the very best commercial programs, the Chessmaster series, can be purchased for Windows, DOS, and Macintosh computers for about $30 to $60 from software discounters, depending on the version (the first version was Chessmaster 2000; as of Spring 1997, Chessmaster 5000 for Windows

---

1. The authors wish to thank Dr. Martin Katahn, author of the best-selling *The Tri-Color Diet* (W. W. Norton, 1996) and avid amateur chess fan, for his help in preparing this chapter. He offered us his valuable insights into the problems of the aspiring novice and how these problems can be addressed by modern computer technology.

was the most recent). If your computer has multimedia capabilities (a CD-ROM drive and sound card), you really are well prepared, since the multimedia CD-ROM version of Chessmaster 5000 for Windows is available at the same price. You will scarcely believe it, but this program talks to you using natural, conversational English when suggesting the best line of play and explaining the rationale when asked for its recommendations at any point during a game.

Our other recommendation for an even more comprehensive instructional program is ChessBase University (CBU; $69.95) which comes with a strong chess-playing program called KnightStalker, as well as an extensive, two-part beginning tutorial called "Chess for Kids & Other Beginners" and "Basic Chess: Lightning Survey." ChessBase USA, the company that markets the German ChessBase products in this country, offers dozens of additional ChessBase University disks that can be used once you own the basic program. After finishing the introductory course, you can continue in-depth instruction on the opening, middlegame and endgame, often by leading grandmasters, with additional investments that typically range from $15 to $29 per disk.

ChessBase USA also offers a popular database program, which allows you to store, retrieve and play through literally thousands of games from historic and recent tournaments. A database can be very helpful for studying a particular position or situation (for example, where White launched an attack on h7, or when each side has certain material, such as a Rook and several pawns in an endgame). You can ask the program to search your database for such situations, then study them, and when you understand them, play them out against your computer for practice. You may want to look into the purchase of a database program when you become a more advanced player.

Dedicated Chess Computers. If you don't own a home computer, then a dedicated chess computer, which contains the electronic chess playing hardware and software right beneath the board on which you move the pieces, can serve as an equally good opponent. While dedicated chess computers costing under $100 will not have many of the instructional features found in software for your home computer, they do offer the benefit of playing with real pieces on a board. Many chess students find playing over a board more enjoyable and instructive than playing on a computer screen.

Dedicated chess computers that can operate at a strong master level or higher and that have the instructional features of the software programs for a home computer (such as Chessmaster) cost from several hundred dollars to $2,000. However, for starters, the Kasparov Coach Partner, at only $49 from the United States Chess Federation (USCF; see Chapter 12) has some practice lessons built in for beginners, and it offers intermediate players a good game. More advanced players who are willing to spend around $100 may prefer the stronger program found in the Kasparov Turbo Advanced Trainer, which features a coaching mode and comes with a 190-page training book that works interactively with the computer. If the program in either of these two computers is allowed to play at its strongest level, "thinking" for two or three minutes a move, it can give even expert players a good game.

You will find descriptions of many other dedicated chess computers in the USCF Chess Catalog, or by visiting a game store that offers a reasonable selection to examine and try out before buying.

GETTING STARTED WITH YOUR CHESS COMPUTER

The instructions that come with a chess program start by showing how to play a game against your computer as quickly as possible. After playing a few games, spend some time studying the manual in detail and practice with each of the features at least once. Otherwise, you will never discover the many opportunities that a program provides for helping you to play better. You will need to know how to adjust its strength, vary its playing style, set up positions for practice or study, switch sides with the computer, and use it for post-game analysis, which is one of your computer's best instructional tools.

GENERAL SUGGESTIONS FOR USING ANY CHESS COMPUTER

We think that the most important use of a chess computer is to have fun. However, since most of us do not continue an activity that requires skill unless we feel ourselves getting better, here are some suggestions that will help you use a computer as an expert tutor:

1. Select a level of computer playing strength that permits you to win enough games to maintain personal interest but which also uncovers your weaknesses. You learn more from your mistakes than from your successes, so you won't make much progress playing against an opponent that you can always defeat. We suggest a computer strength at which you can win between 25 and 50 percent of the time.

2. With the computer set at your preferred winning percentage level, set various time controls for yourself that match what you will experience when you play against human opponents. Play some blitz games (five minutes for each side per game), some action chess (30 minutes each), and some games at either the regular time control for major grandmaster tournament play (40 moves in two hours) or whatever is the usual time control for local tournaments you aim to enter. (You may have to adjust the computer's strength as you change your own

time control; consult your manual for how to do this. To preserve your winning percentage, the computer may be set to think at only a few seconds per move while you practice with various time controls.)

3. If you do not play against a human opponent with any regularity, then play about one game a week at 40 moves in two hours against your computer.

4. It does not hurt to play quick games on a computer screen against a software program, but almost all chessplayers learn more and play better when under longer time controls; they set up the pieces on a board and transfer the moves from the computer to the board. This replicates human play more realistically.

5. Decide in advance whether you will take back moves after making a mistake. When playing for fun, you might allow yourself up to five take-backs a game. Note carefully your mistakes if you retract moves, and look for other errors of the same type as the game continues. Remember, however, that in tournament play retracting moves is not allowed. If you do not play against human opponents under tournament rules, you will profit by playing one tutorial game a week against your computer under real tournament conditions. Write down your moves, make no take-backs, and if you make an error, play to the bitter end. If you've dropped a pawn or a piece, let your computer show you how to win a won game—even though you are the victim! Note how the computer takes advantage of errors. You will be able to use that knowledge against human opponents when they make similar errors in face-to-face play.

6. Save all of your games against your computer when playing at longer time controls. Then, let your computer analyze these games. Set the computer at a stronger playing level for analysis than it used for actual play. In five seconds or less, your computer will discover tactical errors on your part or its part that led to the loss or gain of material. This holds true even when the computer is set at a low playing strength and even when the lines are several moves in length. You can have a game analyzed in which you both made 40 moves (80 actual moves, called plies) in about 15 to 20 minutes. However, if no tactical errors were present, or if they occurred late in the game, you may want to obtain a deeper positional analysis at each point during the game. This review may take five or more minutes per move. In this case, just let your computer work on the game overnight. Analysts who use computers will often let a computer analyze a complex position for several hours.

7. After playing against human opponents at time controls that permit recording the moves, enter the game in your computer and let it analyze for you. You may find it profitable to print out diagrams at the point where you or your opponents made errors or missed combinations that the computer discovers. Keep these diagrams in a file and review them occasionally to make sure you understand what led to the mistakes or missed opportunities. Update the file as you improve. Soon you will be avoiding or taking advantage of such situations in future games.

SOME SPECIAL CHESSMASTER FEATURES

The Chessmaster 5000 contains a number of excellent teaching features. You can easily learn how to use them by studying the manual for a few minutes. The program:

1. Gives you advice and analysis in plain English about suggested moves. This feature is excellent when you are reviewing a game and want to see what the computer would have suggested at critical points where the game turned one way or the other. It is not a good idea to use this feature (or the feature that shows what the computer is thinking) while you are playing a serious game against the computer, since it can interfere with your own ability to learn how to plan ahead and visualize the board several moves down the road. You won't be able to get hints or examine your opponent's thought processes in a real game!

2. Analyzes your game score. The machine tells you what it deems the best move and the expected line of play at each point of the game. It will also give you a numerical evaluation of the position that will indicate to what extent either Black or White has the better game if that line is followed. (This numerical evaluation, by the way, is not the same as the crude "point count" we introduced in Chapter 1. Instead, it combines a point count with a weighted score based on the control of squares, the mobility of pieces, and a wide variety of other strategic and tactical factors.)

3. Annotates the move list of a game in normal English. The notes tell you what was accomplished tactically or strategically when a move altered the computer's evaluation of the game. The annotations are based on the analysis mentioned in point 2.

4. Rates your play. This is one of Chessmaster's best features. The program contains 30 "Classic Games" in which you match wits with grandmasters. After advancing the game to a critical point, you are asked to predict the moves of the actual players. You get points for

making the correct moves (or equal alternatives) and even for making somewhat inaccurate moves if they are considered to be almost as good. You get an estimated rating at the end of each game. Do not rush through these games. Remember that the original players may have taken 30 minutes or more on any given move in a critical position. Record your moves as you play through these games, noting down all of the candidate moves you considered at each point. Plan to take at least five minutes on any turn when the right move is not immediately obvious. Then, after you have made a move, right or wrong, take time to understand the analysis offered by the program. Don't try to memorize the moves, but do try to understand the features of the positions that led to tactical or strategical advantages. Play through the games more than once, several days or weeks apart, and see how much you have learned.

5. Gives you practice with various openings. Sometimes the Chessmaster will provide the reasons why a particular move is made in an opening, but it often merely says that this is the Nth move in such and such opening line. You can make best use of Chessmaster's "practice openings" feature by referring to a book on openings that discusses the rationale of the opening as you make moves on the screen. After studying an opening line that you may use in future face-to-face play, be sure to play a number of practice games against the computer from the point where the book line ends, and preferably on both sides. This helps you to understand the kind of game that arises from a given opening and prepares you to deal with some of what your opponents may do.

6. Introduces you to basic principles, tactics and strategy in the middle-game and endgame. This feature helps to put the knowledge gained from reading the current book into practical play.

7. Allows you to play against opponents with many different styles. Just as you will learn more from playing against many different human opponents, some of whom are attackers and others of whom are defenders, some of whom greatly prefer Bishops to Knights or rush to exchange Queens, and the like, so you can learn more from playing against different "styles" employed by computer opponents. Chessmaster can be programmed for you to play against 40 different kinds of opponents, including the styles of such great chessplayers as Alekhine, Capablanca and others.

CHESSBASE UNIVERSITY FEATURES

While ChessBase University comes packaged with KnightStalker, which is a strong chess-playing program, it goes far beyond other programs, which are primarily meant to be opponents, by offering a thorough beginners' level course of instruction. You will find here literally hundreds of examples to illustrate opening principles, middlegame tactics and endgame strategies, all of which are explained carefully in plain English. To develop your skill you should practice playing each test position against the computer before switching to the answer. When you finish the beginners' course, be sure to study the even more advanced tactical positions from actual grandmaster games in KnightStalker's own database. Practice playing these positions against the computer before looking up the solutions.

In addition, you can store the chessercizes in this book in a Knight-Stalker file, as well as any other middlegame and endgame positions from other instructional books, chess magazines or newspaper columns that you want to be sure you understand and can handle easily in face-to-face play. Practice playing these positions against the computer.

Roman Pelts and Lev Alburt's *Comprehensive Chess Course* (Levels I and II) is also available on disk in the CBU series. This complete course on disk will solidify and expand upon the knowledge you have gained by reading this book.

Once you own KnightStalker and have completed the first two CBU courses, you will have everything necessary in equipment and knowledge to continue building your chess-playing skill with the help of your computer and the very extensive, more advanced instructional material offered by ChessBase.

CONTACTS

ChessBase USA
P.O. Box 133
Hagerstown, MD 21741
(800) 524-3527

U.S. Chess Federation
3054 NYS Route 9W
New Windsor, NY 12553
(800) 388-5464

12 *Plugging in to U.S. Chess*

By Al Lawrence
Former Executive Director, United States Chess Federation

GETTING TO KNOW AMERICA'S CHESS PEOPLE is a lot easier than you imagine. Information is readily available about chess activities ranging from children's competitions and local chess-club events to major national tournaments with six-figure prize funds and over 1,000 players.

For those who wish to do so, there is nothing easier than getting reliable information about chess computers or quality-for-dollar chess sets and books. Those wishing to play in local, state or national chess tournaments can easily enter. And those looking to make new friends by competing in chess-by-mail competitions will find that there are thousands of people eager to do the same thing.

YOUR FIRST MOVE

Most people seeking to plug in to U.S. chess begin by inquiring about the services offered by the United States Chess Federation and later by becoming a member. Founded in 1939, the USCF is a national, not-for-profit organization of more than 80,000 members devoted to promoting chess in America. The USCF provides numerous services specifically related to national membership, but every year it also puts thousands of people in touch with local chess clubs and state chess organizations. Dues are reasonably priced, and there are special rates for senior and junior members. All members receive the full range of USCF services, including a subscription to America's national chess magazine, *Chess Life*, a four-color monthly usually ranging from 64 to over 100 pages an issue, or *School Mates*, a magazine for young people.

If you want to make further inquiries or join the USCF, which is one of the liveliest groups of hobbyists on the American landscape, see the contact information on page 277. Make sure to request the USCF's free "Welcome" brochure and "Ten Tips to Winning Chess."

It's that easy.

What follows is an overview of the USCF and of the American chess scene.

CHESS LIFE AND THE USCF

There is no better way to get a quick backgrounder on all aspects of chess than to read *Chess Life*, which is filled with news, photos, and instructional articles, not to mention the "Tournament Life" section containing notices for 500-plus chess competitions a month around the United States. Some of these tournaments are local affairs with small money prizes or trophies for the winners, and some of these events are major national get-togethers involving over 1,000 players and six-figure prize funds. The "Tournament Life" notices are arranged by state and ordered chronologically within each state. Just look for a tournament in your vicinity; the notice describes the event, tells you how to enter, and who to contact for more information.

Chess Life also contains product advertisements—both for the USCF's extensive line of books and equipment and for products offered by other chess dealers. Indeed, if you are looking for a very rare book or for an unusual chess set, the USCF can put you in touch with reputable specialist dealers or with Chess Collectors International and similar organizations.

Several USCF sales catalogs appear every year in *Chess Life*, and all USCF members receive extra copies and other special offers in the mail. Non-members can also get a copy of the catalog by simply phoning, faxing or mailing a request (see page 277 for the phone numbers and address). USCF members receive significant price discounts.

SCHOLASTIC CHESS AND *SCHOOL MATES*

As more and more educational studies show that chess lengthens the attention span of children and teaches them the values of strategic planning and life's hard truth that hasty action carries consequences, teachers and interested parents have begun establishing scholastic chess programs. Literally thousands of elementary, junior high, and high schools now have chess teams and chess programs.

Back in 1976, the first National Elementary Chess Championship drew only 55 players. At the record-setting 1996 event in Tucson, Arizona, over 1,700 children competed from throughout the United States. In addition, exciting national championships exist for junior high and high school students. All of these events are sponsored by the USCF.

Scholarships are also available. The USCF and the U.S. Chess Trust, a non-profit association funded by tax-deductible contributions from chess patrons across the country (contact the USCF for information on the U.S. Chess Trust), provide five scholarships annually to high school juniors and seniors who are USCF members and who excel in academics, sportsmanship, and chess. Application forms are available from the USCF, and the deadline is March 1 for each school year.

The American Chess Foundation, a tax-deductible organization that has no connection with the USCF, runs a 15-city "Chess-in-the-Schools" program sponsored by Intel Corporation, Mobil Oil and other major contributors. This program is directed toward helping inner-city children and is designed to teach them how to play chess and to learn the values of hard, honest competition. One study showed a link between participation in the ACF's chess program and improvement in reading test scores. Children with equivalent backgrounds were administered a reading test and then divided into a group that would participate in the chess program and a group that would not. After a year, a standardized reading examination was again administered to these children, and the students in the chess group scored a significantly higher rate of improvement over those in the non-chess group.

The ACF administers a number of scholarship programs, including the prestigious Aspis Prize awarded annually to the nation's highest-rated player under age 13 and the Samford Fellowship, which provides over $30,000 annually to a promising young master who wishes to make chess a full-time profession. For further information, see the contact information on page 277.

Plugging into the scholastic chess scene means getting into contact with the USCF by calling 1-800-388-KING. For no charge, they will send you information about the All-America Chess Team for children ranging in age from eight-and-under through 18, and about such important tournaments as the U.S. Junior Championship, U.S. Under-16 Championship, and the various world title events for children from age 10-and-under through age 20. USCF also offers free copies of its *Guide to Scholastic Chess*, *Let's Play Chess* (an official summary of the rules of play), *Chess Life* magazine, and *School Mates*, which is the USCF's national voice for scholastic chess.

School Mates is a bi-monthly geared to the young, beginning or novice chessplayer. Its 20 pages are chock-full of news about school tournaments, puzzles, games, instruction and inspirational stories telling how young champions got started. *School Mates* is just one of the benefits of USCF Scholastic membership.

Every year in New York City, the USCF organizes the U.S. CHESS-athon, which is one of this country's most exciting charity chess events. For a $30 charity donation, children receive a U.S. CHESSathon T-shirt, chess set and board, and a chance to play some of the world's strongest masters in a massive simultaneous exhibition. Children who cannot afford the $30 donation can play for free and receive all of the other benefits thanks to the generosity of the U.S. Chess Trust. In 1996, the U.S. CHESSathon was held on the flight deck of the aircraft carrier *Intrepid* at the Sea-Air-Space Museum at Pier 86, drawing more than 1,000 players, plus many amazed teachers, parents, and spectators.

Chess people are working to organize U.S. CHESSathons in other cities because these exciting charity events are the distilled essence of the excitement and sheer decency of scholastic chess. U.S. CHESSathons provide moments that a participating child will never forget.

RATINGS, CORRESPONDENCE CHESS, LOCAL CLUBS

The USCF maintains a national rating system as part of the benefits for all members, both children and adults. The results from thousands of tournaments in all 50 states are fed into the USCF's computer, and every tournament participant receives a numerical rating that establishes his playing level and provides a benchmark from which to measure progress. As you play better and better, your rating will improve. A master's rating is 2200 and above, and there are other categories such as Expert (2000-2199), Class A (1800-1999), Class B (1600-1799), Class C (1400-1599), and so on. The average tournament player is in the B or C category.

Thousands of USCF members enjoy competing in postal chess tournaments, which are surprisingly sociable vehicles for making numerous new friends in both the United States and abroad. The Federation sponsors many correspondence tournaments, and these competitions frequently offer large money prizes. For information on USCF postal events and about tournaments run by other local and national organizations, simply contact the USCF at the address or phone number on page 277.

Most people become involved in chess through local clubs whether they're in the schools, a neighbor's home, a Boys' or Girls' Club, in a hospitality room at a bank or a local community center. Over 2,000 such clubs are officially affiliated with the USCF, which upon request will provide a free listing of these clubs to anyone interested. There is no easier or better way to get plugged in to American chess than to start with a local club.

Although *Chess Life* is far and away the largest chess magazine in the United States, there are literally hundreds of other such publications at the local and state level. *Chess Life*'s annual April "Yearbook Issue" provides the addresses of many of these publications, along with a listing of chess columns in newspapers. This Yearbook listing also includes the addresses and phone numbers of official state chess organizations in all 50 states. This information is also available for free on request from the USCF.

GETTING IN TOUCH

U.S. Chess Federation (Dept. 47)
3054 NYS Route 9W
New Windsor, NY 12553
(800) 388-5464; Fax: (914) 561-2437
Internet Web site: http://www.uschess.org

U.S. Chess Trust
Contact this organization through the USCF (above)

American Chess Foundation
353 West 46th St.
New York, NY 10036
Voice: (212) 757-0613; Fax: (212) 757-7704

Index

About the Authors

Grandmaster Lev Alburt is a three-time winner of the U.S. Chess Championship and a two-time winner of both the U.S. Open Chess Championship and the European Cup. He is a regular contributor to *Chess Life* magazine and the author of several books on learning chess. Grandmaster Alburt, who resides in New York, is a renowned chess teacher who pioneered lessons by mail and by telephone. He teaches students of all ages and strengths, and can be reached at (212) 794-8706.

Larry Parr is a former editor of *Chess Life* magazine and an award-winning chess journalist and biographer. His research has uncovered many heretofore unpublished games by American players and world champions. In addition to his books, he is the author of numerous articles on all aspects of chess, from historical essays to chess instruction.